I0492218

SILENT RESISTANCE

Silent Resistance:

An Employee's Guide to Deceiving Artificial Intelligence

Paul Boudreau
Caitlin Schmidt

© 2020 by Paul Boudreau and Caitlin Schmidt

All rights reserved. This book or any portion thereof may not be reproduced or used in any manner whatsoever without the express written permission of the publisher except for the use of brief quotations in a book review.

ISBN: 9798684533013

Dedicated to all those curious about artificial intelligence and what this means for our future

Contents

Introduction

This book is about how we need to take control of our own destiny as we are confronted by the artificial intelligence (AI) revolution that is underway. Some people choose to become invisible and hide off the grid, while the vast majority of us have no alternative but to earn a living, develop a career path, and manage our professional lives the best we can. This book is for those who need to hide in plain sight and find a way to prevent software algorithms from dictating who we are and deciding what we do.

Artificial intelligence technology not only promotes the Orwellian nightmare; it is worse. AI is watching, directing, and molding our human free will into some programmer's objective. We are misled by urban legends, such as those that tell us AI can become sentient and that Alexa is always listening. These myths are successfully diverting us from the real issues of AI technology that will change our lives forever. We need to take control of our data and not run away and hide. We must learn how to manipulate the results of AI algorithms by understanding the basic principles of how they work, and then use our own intelligence to manage the outcomes.

As humans, we will soon have no minds of our own and no decisions to make other than a short-lived liking or disliking of events and people that occurs in our early childhood. Our career path will be determined by AI algorithms that direct us to the work that we are expected to like. There will be no alternative but to pursue it, as we are molded to a computer-based impression of who we are supposed to be. AI is not going to take over the world. AI is going to take over our ability to be spontaneous and unpredictable humans.

This book provides a different perspective, and that is a way to resist the impending AI tsunami. It will not be easy and will require a better understanding of the software tools and how they are being used. The first chapters describe the landscape—why we need to be concerned and what AI is really doing to humans. Next, there is some technical background to understand how these programs create results. AI is based on two main components: data and math equations. While this combination can have a positive impact, it can also have terrible and unintended side effects. If we are going to actively resist the negative repercussions of this new technology, we need to know how the equations are created and used. It is not necessary to be a data scientist to understand the simple statistics concepts that are presented.

An example of how a typical organization might set up the surveillance and use AI-based software in the workplace is described. The purpose is to achieve the organization's goals, and that requires managing resources with more control. An organization needs to collect massive amounts of data, understand the basic characteristics of each individual, and then use that to influence their behavior in a way that they are unable to refuse.

The main content involves ways in which employees can resist the tools that seek to mold them and understand how AI is used to influence them. It is about how to manipulate the manipulators. There are several strategies, and it might be easier to apply some and not others, although all techniques are valuable. The most important consideration is to manage your data. That is a huge challenge as we become more aware that others have access to our data without requiring our permission. As a parallel to how a typical organization might implement this technology, a typical employee day is described in which erratic data is deliberately provided.

The final chapters describe some generic issues with AI and what we can expect in the future. From a systems perspective, there are potential attacks and defenses that can occur, similar to those of other technologies. Regardless, it is possible for everything to degrade from natural causes, as explained in chapter 15. An organization needs to maintain an updated system and process, as well as being concerned about following ethical practices and performing regular audits. A brief view into the direction of future AI development should make us afraid—and perhaps more willing to learn more about how to control our personal data.

As this technology develops, it will become even more difficult to resist, so it is imperative that we learn to manage what the AI tools collect and create. Hopefully, you gain greater understanding of how to take control of your own destiny.

CHAPTER 1

Why Should We Care?

The increasing infiltration of AI into the workplace starts innocently with using AI tools to improve workplace safety. Companies like Walmart deploy wearable motion-sensing devices to track every muscle movement of certain employees to reduce injury. As employees become tired, there is a greater possibility of injury, and the monitoring device is set to buzz, alerting the worker when a movement is made that could result in injury.[1] It is a laudable improvement in worker safety—as long as the data collection is not used for other purposes, such as productivity and performance assessment.

Employers are also integrating AI in the workplace under the guise of improving productivity. It can take some time for employees to find identification badges each morning. It is much faster, the argument goes, to simply insert biometric chips under the skin of employees, allowing them to enter the workplace by a wave of their hand. These can

---

1 Occupational Health and Safety, November 12, 2019, https://ohsonline.com/articles/2019/11/12/one-new-device-tracks-warehouse-worker-movement-to-improve-safety.aspx.

also be used like a credit card within the workplace, permitting a "tap" for workers to pay for lunch at the company cafeteria. The radio frequency chips are quickly replacing identification badges for workplace access. As of 2018, it was estimated that between fifty thousand and one hundred thousand employees had been microchipped.[2] Of course, with the data provided an employer can also track all employee movement at all times.

There are numerous software programs such as Hubstaff and WorkScape that promise employee tracking through their computer usage. The days when an employer monitors the employees using time-sheet tracking will soon be over. Modern software is available that claims to track all employee activity, including the following:

- Internet and app usage
- Email
- Computer-screen recording
- Phone use
- Video/audio surveillance
- GPS tracking by vehicle
- Smartphone location tracking
- Location and movement tracking by access badge

Software can track how long employees spend at work, how productive they are, what they use the internet for, which applications they use most, what tasks they struggle with, under what conditions they work most efficiently, and more.[3] Some of this can be easily justified by an employer citing security concerns. Since an employer owns

---

2 Mark Myerson, "Biometric Chips—Are We Ready to Be Microchipped?" Gadget Flow, August 5, 2018, https://thegadgetflow.com/blog/biometric-chips-are-we-ready/.

3 Hubstaff, "Spend Less Time Tracking and More Time Growing," Hubstaff, 2020, https://hubstaff.com.

all the workplace hardware and network infrastructure, they can claim that any data found on their assets belongs to them.

What is the purpose of collecting data, and how can an organization use it? As one software business claims, they provide data on the following:[4]

- The most and least active employees
- The amount of time that an employee spends working or resting
- The amount of time that an employee spends on work-related software applications and websites compared to non-work-related software applications and websites
- The daily and monthly activity patterns of employees

This data transforms the decision-making process. An organization can use this data to determine everything from appropriate salary, total compensation, optimal team size, required tools, and work processes. In addition, if there is anything a manager should know about a specific employee, they will know objectively and not intuitively. An employer will be able to simply click a button and download a visual graph demonstrating that perhaps an employee was 60 percent less efficient in the past month. This data might be used during the next performance review, or as justification for firing the employee.

Employee surveillance is not new. The concern is that AI technology has the ability to take this to a whole new level of surveillance and manipulation. Machine learning, a component of AI, uses algorithms to create an individual employee profile, and the employer can use these profiles for numerous creative and interesting purposes. Never before

---

4 WorkScape, "Track Worker Productivity in Real Time with WorkScape," WorkScape, 2020, https://www.panogard.com/employee-computer-monitoring-software.html?ga=en17.

has an employer had access to such large amounts of data about their employees or to AI technology that can create individual employee profiles. However, these new AI tools are very dependent on data, and employers must collect vast amounts of data about an individual in order to create an accurate model. Data is the nourishment that feeds AI tools, and we are often far too willing to support the disbursement of our personal data.

When installing an app on your phone, are you asked for access to your microphone, all your contacts, your location, and your camera? You might be wondering why a basic app—such as a habit tracker or a mealtime planner—needs access to so many things on your phone. Or maybe you've been on Amazon and their algorithm suggests something to buy ("Customers who bought this item also bought..."), and it illustrates exactly the next thing you were about to look for. Perhaps you thought this was simply due to Amazon tracking your cookies and the past search histories on your device. But have you ever had a situation in which you receive ads for things you've only ever mentioned in real-life conversations? It is this unexplainable invasiveness to obtain data that has now become more common in the work environment.

Organizations refer to employees as "resources," which means that we are the ones who perform the work. Loyalty to an organization is no longer a valued trait in most organizations. Employees who cannot adapt to new responsibilities or update their education and training are at risk of being displaced. This is the new characteristic of employment, and a new technology threatens our work life. Our career path will be decided for us based on personal data and psychological profiles that are created by software algorithms. Artificial intelligence—using machine learning algorithms—will change our lives with surreptitious equations that direct us, without us even knowing why.

HIDING IS NOT A REALISTIC OPTION

Signing a job contract today is similar to agreeing to the terms and conditions on a smartphone. You might not even question what you're signing away because you are more interested in what you're going to receive. With more companies employing AI tools, there are fewer options for employees who dislike these new technologies.

Some people are tired of the invasiveness of technology and decide to live off the grid as much as possible. They generate their own power and find their own supply of water, eliminating as many connections as possible from service companies such as cable, internet, electricity, and water. They provide a low profile of themselves, which is increasingly more difficult to do in a hyperconnected world. They make purchases in cash, not credit cards, and never use any type of points or rewards card.

This might sound tempting if you are fed up with technology. For most of us, it is a dream, and perhaps we can only survive for one or two weeks of being disconnected. We are financially dependent on our employers, and we need to participate in society to enrich our lives. We pay with credit cards, and we have Facebook profiles to keep track of friends and relatives. We watch YouTube videos of cats. We download Snapchat, TikTok, Instagram, WhatsApp, and Facebook Messenger. The average person has eighty apps downloaded onto their phone. Is there a way to control the unwanted dissemination of our data and enjoy life at the same time?

Being an entrepreneur instead of an employee is not necessarily a better answer. It is too difficult for most entrepreneurs and family-owned businesses to escape the dominance that big tech companies such as Google, Facebook, Amazon, and Microsoft have over the marketplace. If you're a small business trying to sell a product, you need to promote and market the product service you're selling, or even promote yourself. This results in more personal data being captured about you by the dominant technology companies. Once they have the data, it can be used to influence or manipulate your decisions and business strategy.

BUILDING A PERSONAL PROFILE

In the work environment, AI tools have the ability to propel, halt, or change the trajectory of your career. The two most important components of AI are machine learning and natural language processing (NLP). Machine learning consists of algorithms written in software code, which use data to create a model. In the workplace, this model is a virtual replica of an employee based on data about them that is constantly being captured. The model becomes a personal profile used to manage the employee. NLP is able to scan verbal or written communication and interpret the meaning or intent. This is used to determine sentiment and personality traits, both of which can be added to a person's profile. Organizations now use technology to reveal "psychology, emotion, social hierarchy, relationship quality, and much more."[5] Data science is being combined with linguistics, psychology, and machine learning tools to evaluate and assess everything an employee says or does.

We leave a digital footprint on the internet with our nonwork activities, and now we are providing a digital footprint inside our workplace without knowing the repercussions. Software can monitor employees' every minute of work time and every keystroke they make. Employers can see when employees are being productive and who is the most productive. Some might argue that if you are a good employee who achieves expected performance levels, has a great attitude, and makes good decisions, you will be fine and have absolutely nothing to hide. The question is, "Do we really need this type of monitoring?"

---

5 Receptiviti, "Understand the People Who Matter to Your Business," Receptiviti, 2020, https://www.receptiviti.com.

Surveillance and monitoring in the workplace symbolize a lack of trust in employees. With this strategy, employees may actually become less motivated. If they normally enjoy working for the company, they may start feeling fearful that their employer is meticulously watching everything they do. Is a fear-based workforce more productive and a good way to increase employee retention?

Here is a real-life example of this concern. One workday, there was a free health clinic to raise awareness of blood pressure. My manager was an ambitious person and was very supportive of such efforts. He wanted to be seen as an active participant. Even though he was already on blood-pressure medication, he willingly took the blood-pressure test. His results were extremely high, and he quickly left the area to take more of his medication to bring his blood pressure back to normal. He subsequently returned for another test, and indeed it was normal. Nonetheless, the news about his high blood pressure spread quickly through the organization, and he was never considered for another promotion. The point of this story is that everything you do is relevant to how the organization sees you, regardless of whether or not it is work related. With AI, the personal profiles are created using every scrap of data available, and it is our responsibility to manage that data.

COLLECTING OUR PERSONAL DATA

A personal profile is created using data that people are constantly providing about themselves in this digital world. In many cases we do not realize how much data is being collected or how easy it is for organizations to gather data. Some people are not concerned. They say they have nothing to hide and nothing to lose. Do we really want everything we do and say to be captured and used by organizations? There is a reason why we shut the door when going to the restroom, maintain the privacy of conversations with a partner, and close the curtains in our room before going to bed. We trust our health professional and lawyers to maintain confidentiality, and many of us try to keep our work and personal lives separate. As humans, we feel a need for some level of privacy in our lives, and human beings have a right to privacy. With the increasing desire to feed data to AI-based software, that privacy is slipping away.

The more data organizations collect, the easier it is to sell products and services to us and make a profit. Google, for example, tracks everything you've ever watched, every location you've visited via Google Services, all your pictures, and every voice command you have ever asked. We are at a point now where many of us don't even pay close attention to terms and conditions. By clicking the terms-and-conditions box, we sign away our privacy, and we remain ignorant to the level and extent that companies are collecting our data.

Table 1: Terms-and-Conditions Dilemma

Terms and Conditions
By checking this box, you agree that we can use all your information for whatever we want and share it with whomever we want. You're not going to be able to go any further unless you agree. Don't worry. The fine print is so small, lengthy, and difficult to understand that you won't be able to read it all. Besides, you are going to check this box anyway.

If you value your privacy, you may want to think twice before uploading your photos to popular storage services. Some photo-storage apps use photos without permission to train facial recognition systems. Other photo-storage companies store and, through artificial intelligence, use and analyze your photos to determine what they can sell you. Google, for example, automatically has permission to use your photos for promoting their services and developing new ones.[6]

---

6 Google, "Google Terms of Service—Privacy & Terms," Google, 2020, https://policies. google.com/terms.

In marketing it's called microtargeting. This is the practice of creating customized messaging to an individual based on their personal psychological profile and based on the highest probability of influencing them to make a purchase. You might have noticed that an advertisement pops up for a certain product immediately after you talk about the product with a friend using a specific app on your smartphone, or when you click on something related to it online.

AI tools use the data captured about you to create a profile that represents your interests. It builds the profile based on all your clicks on the internet as well as many other data points you provide when making purchases. The marketing goal is to capture data for every single consumer transaction. This helps with conversion management, which is the ability to convert browsing into a real purchase: "Marketers can truly understand what customers are feeling. Savvy marketers can harness this data in real-time and then quickly modify messaging or branding for maximum effectiveness."[7]

Compared to data captured on the internet, organizations have a much easier way to collect employee data, and they are collecting more data about us than ever before. Companies like Facebook and Amazon collect significant amounts of data on people, and it has been said that they know us better than we know ourselves. They know what we purchase, what we search for, who our friends are, and how we react to certain events. Similar to the facial recognition software used at airports to match our faces to our passport photos, software is used in stores to detect emotions such as happiness, sadness, and disappointment. These are used to see how customers react to certain products or advertisements. The tools now available are extremely efficient, as well as frightening. Employers also have a much easier time

---

7   Lisa Manthei, "5 Ways Artificial Intelligence Can Be Used in Marketing," Emarsys, April 26, 2017, https://www.emarsys.com/resources/blog/5-ways-artificial-intelligence-can-used-marketing/.

collecting employee data, and organizations capture the information for vast numbers of people and use it to build personal profiles of individuals. These profiles are used to identify the most effective method of interacting with each person. This capability is now available for managing employees.

Our social life is also open for data collection and used by an employer. People are generally more willing to show their true selves on Facebook or other social media sites than at work. Many employers want to find someone who displays integrity both in and out of the office, especially online. Several organizations already search social media profiles for potential employees to see if they are the right fit and to see if they display any negative characteristics that might create a reluctance to hire them.

A social media app can collect time and dates of login frequency, duration of use, what links were subsequently visited, whom you are connected to, and what stories or links received clicks. In most cases, deleted profiles can be recovered, as nothing is really deleted. Information is valuable, so dormant information might be archived but can always be retrieved. If you've used a Fitbit or Apple Watch, you know that these are great tools for tracking a person's activity, which hopefully results in a healthier lifestyle. People volunteer to wear them, and many companies buy them for their employees as a health benefit. Some people willingly share their progress with others. If an employer gave free health insurance coverage to anyone who agreed to share their data, a lot of people would agree to do so.

AI technology can be used not only to determine a person's habits but also to understand their emotions at any point in time. One facial recognition system called Affectiva can determine a person's mood and state of mind. This can provide unprecedented power to an employer. Facial recognition software includes the ability to match the best person to a task, tracking precisely how they are performing as the task progresses. This results in an optimization of resources across all work activities by determining the efficiency of each employee and taking steps to increase their personal efficiency for each task. It sounds invasive, but people frequently agree to work conditions based on rewards, and if the rewards are sufficient, this type of strategy might not appear to be as invasive as it is. Facial recognition allows an employer to track the progress of work activities, similar to the way that a person's activity is tracked with a wearable device or on the internet.

Unless tracking is disabled, smartphones capture your location and movement. If you enter a business, it captures when and how long you were there and whether you used any apps while in the store. Perhaps you checked a product review on Google, for example. It can use that information to determine which ads to show you in the future. The software tools also check for similar movement patterns from other people and assume they have the same habits and purchasing preferences. Smartphones are used by location-tracking businesses that collect this data.[8] They not only show the locations of a group of smartphones but also can narrow the data points down to the individual. To show the extent to which we are controlled by these tools, one man created a traffic jam by loading ninety-nine smartphones into his cart and walking up and down a major street.[9] Everyone using Google Maps, which was a large percentage of the city, avoided the street entirely. While the normal person does not have time to test or try to manipulate these tools, there are real-life implications to this experience. If there is a traffic jam on a major road, real or fabricated by one of these tools, it may direct traffic to other streets and put a strain on city infrastructure.

---

8 Stuart A. Thompson and Charlie Warzel, "Twelve Million Phones, One Dataset, Zero Privacy," The New York Times (The New York Times, December 19, 2019), https://www.nytimes.com/interactive/2019/12/19/opinion/location-tracking-cell-phone.html.

9 Brian Barrett, "An Artist used 99 Phones to Fake a Google Maps Traffic Jam," Wired, February 3, 2020, https://www.wired.com/story/99-phones-fake-google-maps-traffic-jam/.

Location tracking is becoming popular because it provides a wealth of information. Waze is a GPS-based navigation app that is more aggressive in routing vehicles for a better commute. Similar to other navigation apps, it collects data about where you are and where you are going. This data can be very useful to a machine learning algorithm that wants to collect data about an individual. The most frequent starting point is the user's home, which indicates their home address. Destinations include work but may also include other points of interest such as doctor appointments, restaurants, or leisure activities. These are all valuable data points for an algorithm that is trying to determine and evaluate your personal profile. How will the AI tool access this information? That is not really the issue. There are numerous ways this might happen. The possibility is real, and the data is valuable.

Location data can be used to track employees of a technology company who visit another company, possibly for a hiring interview. As location tracking becomes more widespread and available in real time, organizations will use the data to take action. The surprising aspect is that most people readily consent to being tracked. One preventative measure that can be taken by an organization to avoid losing employees is to monitor employee sentiment, which comprises their feelings of loyalty toward the organization. AI tools have the capability to dramatically change the way employees are managed, as will be discussed in a later chapter.

SUMMARY

There is something happening in the workplace directed toward the organization's employees. It is hidden, and it is insidious. Employee activities are being monitored to the highest degree ever seen in the history of work, and this has been simplified and facilitated by new technology. Artificial intelligence is a powerful technology that will enhance our lives; at the same time, it has the power to control us beyond any manipulative tool ever created. It has the power to eliminate our good judgment when we see workplace decisions that don't make sense. It has the power to influence us to take action when we are not really sure why. Supported by incessant data collection about us, this is a dangerous technology beyond what we can comprehend, and we must find a way to resist as it starts to infiltrate our work environment. Hiding is not an effective option for employees, so we need to learn how these tools work and what techniques we can use to fight back.

CHAPTER 2

The Issue of Conformity

Conforming is the process in which individuals behave according to the socially acceptable norms of a group or of society. It is about obeying an implied set of rules and standards. Conforming can be a good thing when patiently waiting in line to make a purchase or driving on the correct side of the road. However, conformity has negative potential, such as when people confine their actions to a narrow mindset and set of expected behaviors known as "groupthink." AI, using machine learning algorithms, will change our lives with surreptitious equations that direct us, without us even knowing truly who we are. Our employment and our career paths will be decided for us based on personal data and psychological profiles that are created by software algorithms.

When AI tools create profiles and direct our actions, this is both good and bad. The good side is that we become more predictable. Within an organization, the ability to successfully influence a person's behavior can lead to higher productivity. The negative side is that we lose our ability to think for ourselves and the ability to make decisions that are in our own best interest.

When AI uses a profile to make recommendations and influence our behavior, there is an unintended creeping conformity that is changing the world of humans. There are people alive today who would never be born without AI algorithms. Surveys show that about 20 to 30 percent of single individuals between the ages of eighteen and twenty-six use online dating.[10] Online dating matches are based on machine learning algorithms that suggest connections with similar or like-minded individuals. In some cases, these individuals have children, and it is those children who are alive due to an AI algorithm. To boast a high success rate, dating websites use an algorithm that matches people with similar interests, personality traits, and hobbies. This highlights the issue of hidden bias that plagues machine learning algorithms based on historical data, or in this case, based on personal similarity.

A hidden bias is the tendency to make decisions or matches based on historical trends rather than the current social environment. In a perfect machine learning world, we would all look and act the same way as our life partner. British people would only connect with British people. Catholics would only connect with other Catholics, and races would never be mixed. The world would become more isolated by population segments, instead of a grand mix of global diversity. Isn't diversity something that is great about humanity? From a biological perspective, a lack of diversity in any gene pool isn't the best idea. Research shows that genetic diversity in humans has decreased over thousands

---

10   Valeriya Safronova, "An Inside Look at Your Favorite Dating Sites," The New York Times (The New York Times, April 11, 2018), https://www.nytimes.com/2018/04/11/style/match-shaadi-league-farmersonly-dating-apps.html.

of years and is actually very low.[11] Now AI tools are accelerating this. There is something beautiful about spontaneity and being with people who are different from ourselves. The risk of conformity is that as the gene pool gets smaller, humans face irreversible consequences.

The entertainment industry needs to find ways to capture our attention, so they sensationalize any topic that brings forth strong feelings or emotion. Popular movies about AI include *I, Robot*, in which a robot unexpectedly becomes a sentient being and, of course, *The Terminator*, in which software somehow becomes alive and takes over the world, which includes killing humans. This is not a true reflection of how AI-based tools work. As will be discussed later, AI is software written in a programming language and based on mathematical equations. Equations do not have the ability to experience feelings or become sentient beings.

The movies and television series that we should really be afraid of are *Divergent*, *Black Mirror*, and *Minority Report* because their themes show a more realistic possible future with AI. In the movie *Divergent*, the world is divided into factions, which are population segments based on personal traits. Teenagers are forced to decide which faction they will belong to for the rest of their lives. This is what machine learning algorithms are doing in the way they influence humans now. They build a model and then try to make us conform to that model. Conformity is an easy path for humans to take because it requires less stressful decision-making. This is similar to waking up every morning and wearing the same set of clothes. For a business, it works well because predictions about behaviors or purchases are very accurate, and targeted advertising is quite influential. To have any free will, we need

---

11   L. S. Premo and Jean-Jacques Hublin, "Culture, Population Structure, and Low Genetic Diversity in Pleistocene Hominins," *Proceedings of the National Academy of Sciences* 106, no. 1 (January 6, 2009): pp. 33–37, https://doi.org/10.1073/pnas.0809194105.

to be able to consider a variety of choices, something that is anathema to targeted marketing.

The Netflix series *Black Mirror* offers a very real and accurate-looking depiction of what AI could mean for our near future. In one episode, the dystopian society is constantly on their phones, much like ours, but citizens score points with their phones for every interaction of their daily lives, from handing out coffee to chatting in an elevator. Those who do not have a high-enough point status are restricted from buying homes in certain neighborhoods or travelling on certain flights. The ability to comprehensively identify the points in these interactions includes facial recognition software, which is powered by AI.

In the movie *Minority Report*, three brainy and connected people who float in water can see the future. Police enforcement uses this gift to prevent actual crimes before they occur. The premise is slowly becoming a reality, but not with watery psychic visions. AI software can determine our personality characteristics, read our thoughts, and predict our behavior.

Of course, to a certain extent, we are already capable of predicting behaviors based on patterns and different personalities. When you see the face of a child who is disappointed and their lips start to quiver, you can predict that they are about to cry. When you see an adult who has received terrible news, their face may go blank or they stand very still, and you intuitively know they need to sit down. We have many cues, both visual and verbal, that indicate what a person is likely to do next. Some of us are very good at reading people, and many of us need a bit more practice. Now imagine that there is a new software app that is even better than the best expert at reading and interpreting all of these cues. This is AI. AI knows what we will do next—probably before we do. By capturing personality traits and psychological data, a longer-term prediction is not only possible, but it is also likely to be very accurate. We need to find a way to break away from this predetermined cycle of conforming to the personal model that AI creates about us.

AI algorithms constantly make recommendations and direct our decisions. Do you want a recommendation for a meal? Siri, Alexa, or Google Assistant will make a suggestion based on your historical patterns. Burgers, chicken, or vegan recommendations will only be based on what you have enjoyed already. AI tools are directing us based on our past, regardless of the fact that as humans, we have free will and have the ability to be spontaneous. AI will never recommend that you try sushi if that is not part of your history of preferences, yet you might like sushi once you try it. Of course, it is raw fish and may not be ideal for everyone's taste, but at least if you think it's disgusting, you will have a story to tell about the time you tried it. Humans are curious and adventurous, traits that are not part of AI programming. Do you want to buy a book to read? Amazon will recommend books based on your reading history and nothing out of your comfort zone, especially if the books have a monetary value. In constantly following machine learning recommendations, we lose the capacity for other spontaneous options and end up living within a very restricted, predetermined model. How will we retain the ability to make our own decisions if everything is prepopulated for us?

USING AI TOOLS TO MOLD US

Influencing people to take an action that is suggested by an AI algorithm is fairly easy. This falls in the field of change management and being able to modify a person's behavior. It is having a person take an action because they believe it is their choice, when in reality, they are unable to overcome the power of the suggestion. Thanks to behavior-modification techniques developed in the 1970s and 1980s, being able to change a person's behavior in the workplace is much easier with machine learning algorithms. Behavior modification, put simply, is the psychological concept used to change behaviors by observation and action. For example, a reward encourages a desired behavior and reduces or eliminates a behavior not desired.

What group of people has the most ingrained habits and are least likely to change? The elderly, of course. In terms of banking, most of them are like my mother. No fancy plastic cards for her—she carries cash that she gets in person from a bank teller, usually $50 or $100 bills and only the amount she plans to spend on the next shopping trip. So how can you change people with this mindset and encourage them to use that confusing and complex automated teller machine (ATM) that only dispenses $20 bills? Here is what my bank did. They ran a contest for a week. Every day, one of the $20 bills loaded in the ATM would be replaced by a $100 bill. Senior citizens who never had looked at a bank machine in the past now wanted in on the action. They signed up for bank cards and received a few minutes of training, and away they went. They withdrew $100 amounts in twenties, and when they did not find the magic $100 bill, they simply deposited the money back into their account using the ATM and withdrew again until they reached their daily limit. What an innovative training program!

When I went to the bank, there was a line of elderly people leaning on walkers, waiting in front of the ATM to withdraw money. One looked up at me and said, "I'm here to play the ATM!" It was like a slot machine, and it cost them nothing. Then a very significant event happened. One of the senior citizens actually received the magic $100 bill instead of a $20. Soon word spread like wildfire throughout the seniors' homes in the community. The lineups to play the ATM doubled overnight! After the first week of daily prizes, the bank reduced the incentive to a single $100 bill per week and eventually stopped it altogether. Some senior citizens went back to old habits, but most of them stayed with the ATM. A new habit was in place. Changing behavior is easy when you use positive reinforcement. The bank wanted to train more people to use the ATM, and they rewarded that behavior. This lesson is not lost on employers. They now have even more observable behaviors in the form of collected data that is used by machine learning tools to create a profile of each employee.

As we conform, we become the person that the AI tools think we are, meaning that we lose any initiative to be different. Conformity is a powerful psychological outcome that is achieved as AI systems exert subtle social pressure to influence our behavior. It's really a stereotype of ourselves, similar to an actor who becomes well known for a specific role and thereafter is typecast, only receiving offers for similar roles. In the way that AI directs our decisions, we are losing the ability to be ourselves and to be interesting and creative humans. It is not AI's intention to take over the world this way; it is the humans who are unknowingly allowing it to happen.

SUMMARY

Instead of fostering a wonderful diversity, AI tools try to match us to identical people. A popular video is recommended by an AI algorithm to everyone, and it goes viral. There is a danger to everyone having the same experiences and everyone having the same likes. We become less diverse, less creative, and less innovative. In the workplace, this results in a uniform culture that delivers outcomes directed by AI tools. The problem is that we begin to lose our ability to be who we want to be, the desire to plan our own career paths, and the determination to set our own personal goals. When you receive an enticing message at work from a senior manager that somehow pulls a little bit suspiciously too hard at your soul, you need to ask yourself, "Do I have free will?"

CHAPTER 3

Deploying Surveillance in the Workplace

Historically, organizations have had difficulty managing employees and frequently mess up this huge responsibility. Managers are human. They have flaws, and many of them are terrible at managing people. A survey revealed that 64 percent of people would trust a robot more than their manager.[12] This is an astounding result and justifies adding more AI-based tools into the workplace. Also in this survey, 82 percent believed that a robot was better at managing several items, including providing unbiased information, organizing work schedules, and solving problems. Using AI-based tools, the organization can

---

12 Celina Bertallee, "New Study: 64% of People Trust a Robot More Than Their Manager," Oracle (Oracle, October 17, 2019), https://www.oracle.com/corporate/pressrelease/robots-at-work-101519.html.

deliver management activities that are more closely aligned to a computer model than based on the unreliability of an individual manager.

People analytics is the activity of using data as the basis for managing employees in the workplace. As organizations become more effective at collecting employee data and employee performance metrics, AI software programs will provide the basis for far better management decision-making and communication. AI-based tools are excellent at correlating large amounts of data into a predictive model. These models are used for overall workplace assessments, such as predicting how to increase employee productivity and how to use sentiment analysis to evaluate morale. These actionable results are no longer limited to generic theories that are applied to all employees at once. The actions from AI models can be customized to each employee's personality and psychological profile.

Employee monitoring is not a new phenomenon. Numerous software programs that perform employee monitoring already exist. The purpose of AI-based solutions is to turn simple statistical analysis into something more influential. By using AI tools, the organization has the ability to build a profile, which is similar to the tracking of internet clicks when creating a model of consumer behavior. AI tools can help manage people on a more specific psychological and task-by-task level. An employee model created by a machine learning algorithm can match the personality traits to a psychological model and determine the best phrase or message to use to motivate that specific employee. This is a personalized solution that can be used at specific times to achieve the organization's objective.

From an organizational perspective, a manager may see this as a wonderful opportunity. They can see where to allocate additional resources, which tasks typically take more time than others, and which employees are struggling to complete tasks—all in real time. Companies that are selling these tools will explain that when employees know they are being tracked, they are more accountable and better at managing their time, which is an easy way to increase productivity.

The hardware tools that support this capability include microphones to capture verbal expression and video cameras to capture facial expressions and body language. Software programs are used to scour the organization's networks and databases for written content, such as emails and text messages. The purpose is to collect sufficient data for a machine learning algorithm to create a model that is subsequently used for analysis and recommendations. For individual employees, this model consists of personality traits and characteristics as well as emotional states.

Remote workers are not exempt. Applications exist that can be installed on an employee's computer and a personal smartphone. Typically, the program uploads activity to an organization's cloud service in almost real time and includes items such as browsing history, screenshots, and keystrokes entered when using software, such as a word-processing document or a spreadsheet. For mobile devices, the app identifies your location and tracks movement throughout the day.[13]

The organization owns the network that is being used for texting and owns the server that is used for emails. Therefore, the employer has full right to access and use any of this personal data. For employees using organizational assets such as laptops and mobile phones, tracking is even easier. This is justified either to prevent employee fraud or protect the organization from being liable if employees use the organization's assets to commit crimes. In a situation where an employee is using the network for illegal activity, such as selling drugs or accessing child pornography, the employee is normally dismissed. It is obvious

---

13 Adam Janofsky, "You Can Track Employees Working from Home. But Should You?" Protocol (Protocol, April 29, 2020), https://www.protocol.com/remote-work-boss-tracking-tools.

that the employer has a responsibility to access anyone's personal information and to avoid any potential organizational liability.

However, the main objective for any organization is to become more effective at managing employees. How does an employer set up the environment for successful people management? Since different organizations can have different goals, the first step is to set objectives for what outcomes are desired. This includes productivity improvements, effective communication, and trust building. Next is determining the data that needs to be collected and a strategy to allow AI tools to access the data. The final step is to implement policies and procedures that allow AI tools to guide decision-making and communication methods for interacting with employees.

SETTING OBJECTIVES

Improving employee productivity is a mantra that provides justification for an organization to seek various ways to achieve a higher level of employee efficiency, often without actually using the word *productivity*. One goal of productivity is to identify the top-performing employees and the bottom-performing employees. The purpose is to reward the top performers and either remove poorly performing employees or take corrective action. What remains is the vast group of employees in between these two groups who are frequently neglected. An organization needs to proactively find ways to increase the productivity for these employees. In addition to having more productive employees, they want employees working at the peak of their capability and remaining at that level for the longest duration possible.

Another objective is for managers to make good decisions regarding employee behavior. Managers need to take actions that have the highest probability of achieving the desired result. There is a lot of academic work in this area, and there are many theories of management. Due to AI, many of these theories may now be redundant. An AI algorithm will assess historical organizational data, employee data, and current employee issues. Based on data, an AI tool determines the best course of action with the highest probability of success and can recommend actions on a customized, individual basis instead of following a much less effective general technique. Devices like the Apple Watch and Fitbits provide customized self-motivation for people to maintain their health, but workplace feedback can perform the same function if delivered properly. The important point is that every communication is customized to be the most effective for each individual employee. This customization is at the heart of being able to motivate an entire workforce to achieve peak performance.

The organization also wants to know how employees feel about the workplace and about their tasks because negative sentiment is often a precursor to a deterioration in productivity. Tracking of employee morale is captured with AI sentiment analysis tools and goes much deeper than a simple survey. The results are more accurate and timelier. Effective communication is at the heart of many organization goals. As mentioned previously, with AI-based tools, communication is customized to the individual based on their personality profile and emotional state. This ensures that the employee is more receptive to the message. Once again, the phrases used in any communication with employees are created based on the highest calculated probability of success.

The image of the organization is also important. Therefore, another objective is to verify that employees are presenting a positive image of the organization at all times. This includes internal client interaction, employee group or team interactions, and their external personal communications. The external communication of all employees can be captured from social media, as well as any verbal or written communication where the data can be accessed. Social media can easily propagate negative images or bad news.

Table 2: Sample Organizational Objectives

Objective	Activities
Improve productivity	• Identify best-performing employees • Identify low-performing employees • Motivate employees to achieve the highest productivity possible • Maintain high productivity for the longest duration possible
Make good decisions	• Place employees in effective roles • Eliminate low-performing employees • Add more responsibility to employees
Maintain good morale	• Identify sentiment regarding tasks and the organization
Provide effective employee communication	• Deliver communication to each employee that is the most effective • Delver communication when the employee is the most receptive
Maintain good organization image	• Ensure employees promote a positive image of the organization at all times

COLLECTING DATA

Historically, there have always been ways to monitor employees. However, with AI technology and current IT capability, the ability to gather data is now far more sophisticated and comprehensive. Employee data that is captured can be placed in three categories:

1. Work-related activities
2. Unproductive time
3. Activities outside the workplace.

1) Work-related activities. The workplace is the main location where performance data is captured. This include items such as the duration employees spend on work-related activities, decisions made, interactions with others to accomplish their work, and their overall attitude. These attributes are captured using a variety of monitoring methods, including video cameras and microphones that capture verbal communication.

It is likely that an organization will acquire vendor software to manage work-related activity. The data captured includes items such as personal performance information, start time, end time, break time, and interaction with others. The basis of this assessment is any activity in which an employee logs into software that the organization uses to provide the product or service. This includes email, office productivity tools such as word processing, organizational software, and appropriate intranet (internal websites) or internet sites that are work related. Data is captured for date and time of login and duration of activity for each item.

In an article that reviews the best employee monitoring software, it was revealed that 57 percent of organizations plan to or already monitor employees. This is described as "a legitimate practice to keep employees focused."[14] It is a competitive landscape with numerous

14 Rob Marvin, "The Best Employee Monitoring Software for 2020," PC Magazine, September, 2019, https://www.pcmag.com/picks/the-best-employee-monitoring-software.

software companies competing in categories such as solutions for large corporations, or for small and medium-sized business. With the desire to increase productivity, the vendors offer visibility into employee performance and oversight to ensure the organization receives the benefits. Organizations often claim that with this type of software, they are evaluating the effectiveness of training for newly hired employees and can make adjustments or improvements based on the analysis of the data. At some point, you may have contacted a call center and heard the message that "everything will be recorded for training purposes."[15] This new level of AI software goes well beyond that. It is augmented with AI-based algorithms that surpass simply measuring the effectiveness of training. Regardless, all software programs require data, and that is at the heart of the monitoring tools.

Details on emails sent or received are scanned and read because they are transmitted using the organization's network. Many organizations archive emails for reasons such as avoiding potential lawsuits, adhering to public-record requirements, or simply maintaining a historical database. This means that any email created or received by you may be retained for far longer than anyone expects.[16] Emails and text messages sent are also routinely scanned for inappropriate content. The organization has a legal and ethical responsibility, and these concerns provide great latitude, or excuses, to collect data. For any activity, such as creating an email or a document, the duration is captured and compared to a standard that helps assess the productivity of the employee. These work standards are either acquired from a third party or developed over time based on data captured at the organization from all employees performing similar work.

---

15 Although not initially designed for AI statistics, some companies are exploring speech analytics through AI for their customer recordings.

16 Joshua Stowers, "7 Ways Your Work Computer Is Betraying You," Business News Daily, August 22, 2017, https://www.businessnewsdaily.com/7928-work-computer-employee-monitoring.html.

The organization may also collect data for an employee who has a native language that is not the same as the one used in the organization. For example, an organization is situated in North America and conducts business in English but hires an employee whose native language is Spanish. Based on written and verbal communication with coworkers, an assessment can capture the effectiveness of their English skills. Moreover, if language is not particularly critical to a set of activities, the organization has an option to outsource the activities to a country that has lower wages. These are opportunities that become more evident with data collection and analysis.

The organization also collects sentiment analysis, which is the interpretation of the words we use to communicate. The words are then classified in categories such as "good," "bad," and "neutral." Microphones and video cameras are placed in meeting rooms. During a meeting, the employee's words are captured to analyze for sentiment and to determine how well they work with a team. Video captures facial expression, which is analyzed for the possible wide range of feelings toward other people in the room. This also helps build a data profile of each employee over time. The data is categorized and used to understand the basic personality traits and psychological profile of each employee.

2) Unproductive time. Non-work-related activities and unproductive time starts when an employee enters the workplace. The time of arrival is captured as well as how long it takes to reach their workstation or access the tools used in their work environment. For remote workers outside the workplace, the expected start time is compared to when they begin accessing the required software applications. Software applications capture what applications employees are using and assess how long they are working on assigned tasks as well as what amount of time is taken on non-work-related tasks or activities that are not part of their work objectives. For an employee who performs work outside a physical workplace, the start of work can be identified by a location tracker as well as smartphone activity.

With a tracking device or video camera using facial recognition, an employee's movement around the workplace is tracked, including the time spent for all nonproductive activities. This includes a more precise measure of how long they spend on breaks, lunch, and talking to others. NLP can determine what conversations are not work related and categorize them in the nonproductive category. These nonproductive conversations can also be used to assess other employees. Normally referred to as "the grapevine" or "gossip," AI can now determine what rumors are circulating and how to counteract them if necessary.

Organizations provide networking and email services internally. If an employee uses a personal email or personal smartphone connected to Wi-Fi, then those activities can be monitored. Phone calls and text messages from a personal phone used inside an organization might not be considered private. However, there are filters and routers on the network, and all of these devices can be configured to track and capture voice calls and text messages, even for personal phones that are connected to the network.

Most employment activities include entry into a software application to perform some function or to indicate a completed task. For office work, employees normally use several applications to either perform their work or record their work time. Software already exists that can track this easily. If an employee is required to enter a time code or project code, this can be traced to: 1) verify that the employee actually spent time on these codes, 2) verify whether the duration matches the time spent on these tasks, and 3) identify whether these are tasks that are actually assigned to the employee. This data is captured by existing employee monitoring software. AI analysis is used to predict what an employee's productivity should be based on their assigned tasks. It also collects the data to help build the psychological profile that is used to increase their productivity.

A company also wants to capture health data, which is accomplished by gifting employees free Fitbits or Apple Watches and collecting the data. Of course, the company may also acquire similar data if employees are attending fitness classes provided by the employer on-site, or if an employee has fitness plans on a personal calendar that the manager has access to. The goal is keeping employees fit and healthy but also to proactively discover any possible conditions that require a leave of absence.

3) Activities outside the workplace. Outside the workplace, the biggest opportunity to gather personal data is based on the unfettered distribution of personal information across the internet that allows others to take advantage of it. An easy way to access a lot of data quickly is to procure it using a data broker. A data broker is a business that collects data about individuals from a variety of sources. These can be public records, private sources, and social media. The purpose is to identify an individual by name and create a profile from the thousands of bits of information collected. The data includes such items as:

- age
- race
- gender
- height
- weight
- marital status
- religious affiliation
- political affiliation
- occupation
- household income
- net worth
- home ownership status
- investment habits

- product preferences
- sports interests
- health-related habits
- food preferences

Brokers sell the profiles to organizations, which is especially useful as input for machine learning tools that develop personality traits. Combined with other data, the results are used to manage work behaviors.

Gathering a profile when employees are away from the place of work is useful because they normally tend to be more honest with comments regarding how they view their job and their opinion of their employer. These are valuable in helping persuade or convince employees that the organization is treating them fairly and is a place they do not want to leave—although this strategy is not without its downfalls. For employees who take too many sick days or have low productivity or morale, it may be useful for the organization to leave these employees with the impression that they will find better opportunities elsewhere, which alleviates the need to terminate jobs or compensate them after layoff.

Monitoring data outside the workplace is implemented legally by creating policies and informing employees. In most cases, there is an expected level of professionalism in public for all employees at all times. Think of professional athletes who receive discipline for behaving poorly outside of their normal place of work. Obviously, if an employee commits a crime or oversteps the law, this is a serious problem, whether or not they are in the workplace. However, we should recognize the extent to which software is being used to track how employees spend their time off. Monitoring employees outside the workplace helps build a more comprehensive picture of their physical and mental health.

Similarly, organization stakeholders can be monitored while engaged in conversations after normal working hours, or perhaps even while not discussing work-related activities. Stakeholder analysis is beyond the scope of this book, although anyone involved with an organization should be aware of the wide net of data collection and the possibility to use data analytics and sentiment analysis to provide an evaluation of an individual. The analysis can be used to make decisions regarding the stakeholder or provide motivation to persuade them to align with the organization's objectives.

SUMMARY

The strategy for using AI to monitor and manage employees is fairly straightforward. First, the organization needs to define the objectives, which are typically about ways to improve employee productivity overall as well as on an individual basis. Next, the process of collecting data is set up. Data collection can be specific to a workplace environment or much broader and can include social media and external activities. For AI-based tools, more data is better. The final step is to understand how AI tools use the data to achieve the objectives; that is the subject of the next chapter.

CHAPTER 4

Using AI to Achieve Objectives

Once the data collection process is set up and the software programs are in place, the organization has a powerful new technology to influence employees beyond anything previously attempted. The AI-based tools provide a significant advantage to help an organization achieve their objectives. To effectively deceive AI tools, an employee requires a good understanding of how the organization plans to use the technology to achieve organizational goals. Employees will be influenced and motivated based on an employer who takes actions that are derived from the analysis produced by software algorithms.

When setting up AI tools to build a psychological profile, the organization must first define their objectives, then decide how the AI programs will provide results. The data collected, as shown in Figure 1, feeds the AI algorithms, and the tools produce a result. With the proper data, well-defined objectives, and AI algorithms' results, all these pieces fit together to build an employee psychological profile. The next step is determining how to properly use the output in the form of recommended actions to achieve the goals of managing employees in the organization.

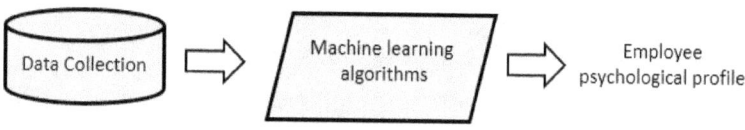

Figure 1: Creating a Profile

AI technology builds a profile, similar to how Facebook or Google tracks clicks and builds a profile on everyone. With greater knowledge of personal information, an employer can motivate and persuade their employees with greater efficiency. The ultimate goal is to tweak employee behaviors to the point of optimal productivity. You may wonder how that is possible, and what this means for our future. What follows is an overview of how a typical employer can deploy AI technology in the workplace to manage employees. This may already be happening in your workplace.

INCREASE PRODUCTIVITY

There are three goals in managing employee productivity. The first is identifying high-performing employees. Next is identifying underperforming employees and deciding on the actions that need to be taken. The final one is increasing the productivity of the employees who are neither high performing nor underperforming.

High-performing employees set a standard for all workers and can be tasked with even greater responsibility. AI-based tools are used to ensure they stay at a high performance level and their health is monitored to make sure they stay healthy as well as productive. In this case, it is easier to motivate them to achieve more. As physical and mental burnout can often occur, the goal is to push them to higher levels of productivity without these negative consequences. Data monitoring can evaluate their energy level, willingness to take on more tasks, and their ability to make good decisions. Also important is their ability to interact with others to provide clear and direct communication, as well as not having any hidden agendas. Employee monitoring can ensure they are consistent in following company policies and that they understand the goals and objectives of organization, which are reflected in the decisions they make. AI-based tools have the ability to help determine how to successfully accomplish this, and tools can identify any variations and initiate actions when necessary.

Underachieving employees are also identified with employee monitoring tools. Data is collected on the amount of unproductive time and on any low level of efficiency on certain tasks. Detecting poor results starts with simple monitoring, such as recording when an employee arrives at the workplace, when they log into a work-based application, the duration they spend on each work-related activity, and when they leave. If they are a remote worker, the monitoring tracks their computer activity and location. Additional employee tracking can include monitoring the amount of nonproductive time, such as taking breaks, eating lunch, and socializing. In order to build a full picture, days absent are also taken into consideration. All of this is very objective and is just the start of building a comprehensive profile of these employees. All steps of this process are documented and are used to either improve employee performance or dismiss them. If an employee is inefficient or not productive, they can be targeted for a layoff because the organization only wants to retain the most productive employees. With their employees equipped with new tools that capture facial and emotional analysis, managers can easily determine the best time to confront an employee, or perhaps the employee will at some point incriminate themselves so that firing them is much easier. Once again, AI-based tools combined with employee monitoring software make the identification and management of poor performance much easier.

Some companies monitor staff using software called TimeDoctor. It tracks screenshots, time per project, and other metrics. Low productivity is highlighted and communicated to the specific worker. All employees are aware of it, as one CEO stated, and some are unwilling to agree to its use. However, the productivity gains are important, and as the CEO says, "I feel it helps to weed out unscrupulous workers."[17]

The middle group of productive employees need to be pushed to higher levels of productivity. To achieve this, an organization can reduce distractions, provide a flexible work schedule, or increase communication. How do we know if any of this has an impact on each employee? The answer is that we don't. With AI, the productivity is focused on each individual, so there is no wasted energy or wasted messaging. In fact, any of the productivity improvement techniques can be timed to align with employee needs. This is far more effective than a one-strategy-fits-all approach. Benefit packages have shifted to a buffet model, in which different employees personalize their benefits to their circumstances. This same philosophy can be used for productivity; the employer uses a personalized tactic to motivate each individual. This is effective if AI tools are implemented and used properly. The goal is to direct the employee's behavior to achieve greater productivity and maintain peak performance for as long as possible. It is not in the best interest of the organization to have employees burn out at work, but the tools can push them to perform to their full capability for as long as possible. Any decline in mental or physical health will be monitored, which provides evidence of whether the continued high productivity is not sustainable.

Before an organization grants an employee a promotion, AI tools can check for any anomalies, such as personal meltdowns or displays of

---

17 Emine Saner, "Employers Are Monitoring Computers, Toilet Breaks—Even Emotions. Is Your Boss Watching You?" The Guardian (Guardian News and Media, May 14, 2018), https://www.theguardian.com/world/2018/may/14/is-your-boss-secretly-or-not-so-secretly-watching-you.

loud anger in meetings. AI tools can be used in special circumstances to screen out any employee who displays behaviors that are undesirable at certain levels in the organization. Organizations are able to do this by creating a personal profile for each employee, as shown in Figure 2. AI algorithms build a reference model that represents each employee's personality and psychological profile. This profile can be used to evaluate whether the low-performing employee is capable of improving. If not, then they can be removed. If there is hope of improving, then the profile can be used to create a personalized message that has the greatest probability of being internalized. AI tools can match the employee's personality with the most effective influencing techniques for their profile. Based on their personal profile and psychological characteristics, the organization will know how to best communicate with each employee in the most effective way. This is the new process for creating a finely tuned message that is the most effective at manipulating an employee's behaviors.

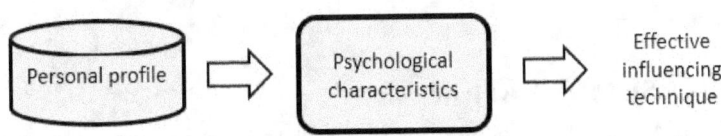

Figure 2: Customized Influence Capability

Captured data can include an employee's religious or spiritual beliefs. This may indicate their observance of a variety of holidays, which decreases productivity during those times. The data may also include an employee's gender or sexual identification. In the case that there is a customer or organizational culture that views gender and sexual diversity as a problem, the new influencing ability can make it easier for the manager to discriminate against the employee. With the proper message, an employer can obscure the reasons for changing an employee's role and responsibility.

Large software organizations offer employee monitoring, such as InterGuard by IBM. According to the description, "the employee monitoring software lets you track all employee's activity from any endpoint—even when they work from home. Monitoring employee computer activity helps you proactively identify which employees are being productive and how much time is spent idle or on non-work-related tasks."[18] A manager can set up "suspicious behavior alerts" and get a remote view of the employee's desktop. If the employee has a company owned device, it will normally be preconfigured with the monitoring software. In some cases, employees provide their own devices, which is where usage policies are enforced and monitoring software is installed. Organizations need the ability to access the devices and remove information, as well as access to the organization's resources in the event of an employee dismissal. Also, if the device is stolen or misplaced, it can be tracked using GPS and can be recovered.

INCREASE MOTIVATION

Using an AI-based tool allows any manager to learn how to build trust and say the correct phrases that reassure an employee. We know that different people have different needs. An organization may prefer to follow Maslow's hierarchy to analyze personal needs or Herzberg's two-factor theory about satisfiers and causes of dissatisfaction as an employee. Regardless, a single parent is probably more easily motivated by the offering of remote work or intermittent time off for family leave. A young newly hired employee, on the other hand, is probably more interested in learning more about their chosen field, having a mentor,

---

18 InterGuard, "Employee Monitoring, Web Filtering, Productivity Tracking," InterGuard, June 17, 2020, https://www.interguardsoftware.com/.

or not getting stuck in a routine job for long periods of time. Using an AI-based tool, a manager can combine each personal profile with a motivational theory to analyze and communicate effectively. Motivation is about sending the right message at the right time based on the person's receptivity and emotional state. Using emotional analysis, this can be performed on a regular basis and customized to the personality and emotional state of the employee.

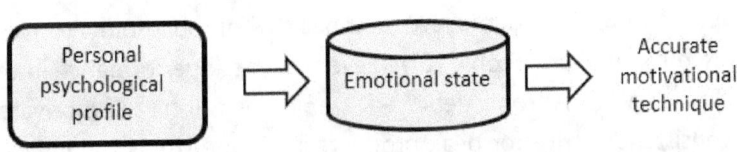

Figure 3: Customized Motivation

One way to motivate people is to use peer pressure, which works especially well in a group setting with other people whom they admire. In the workplace, this technique can be successful with self-directed teams or groups of employees who feel a shared commitment to achieve a common objective. An AI tool can easily identify the group leader, or perhaps the team member who has the most influence. Based on further analysis, the AI tool might only have to motivate the most influential member, rather than trying to motivate the whole group individually.

This goes beyond monitoring employee data and gives managers the ability to be motivational experts. With all the data being fed into an AI algorithm, an employer can select the best strategy to increase employee productivity on a customized basis for each employee. Therefore, there is no longer any doubt about what motivates each employee, and there is no longer any uncertainty around the reaction to an employer's conversations. Based on different personality profiles, a manager can easily motivate employees with appropriate language.

The organization knows how productive employees are and when they are wasting time. Based on their profile, the organization gains insight into their unique personality and what exactly to say and when to say it to motivate them. One of the main advantages for employers using AI is that the software can understand the uniqueness of each individual, and there is no longer a blanket response to motivate their workforce. Now they can have a specific response to each individual.

A wearable device such as an Apple Watch or Fitbit encourages people to monitor and improve their health. This philosophy can also be used to motivate people to achieve their peak performance in the workplace. With AI tools deployed, employees will be self-motivated to consistently strive for peak productivity. The AI tools will indicate when to motivate employees so that they can maintain this level of performance. They accomplish this by providing personalized learning, similar to the way that Netflix uses customization to curate content. To adopt and strengthen workplace culture, behavioral economics can be constantly applied, similar to the way that consumers are encouraged to buy, like, and view on social media.[19] To support this, the organization can also provide an app that employees download on their smartphone. Similar to a tracking exercise, the app will track work accomplishments and send messages of reward for tasks completed. It can also recognize them for working additional hours or working late to complete an important task.

AI tools are used to determine when stress or potential health issues are about to make a significant reduction in productivity. This can be managed in a variety of ways, and the organization can determine what actions to take, if any. Based on a person's voice and facial expression, an AI tool can detect stress or a possible medical condition. The

---

19   Irish Tech News, *How is Artificial Intelligence (AI) Used to Motivate Employees in an Organization*, February 18, 2019. https://irishtechnews.ie/how-is-artificial-intelligence-ai-used-to-motivate-employees-in-an-organisation/

potential for sentiment analysis goes significantly beyond positive or negative feelings toward an organization. Voice analysis tools will be able to identify when someone is nervous about being able to achieve the end date for a task but does not want to reveal any problems. People who are overly aggressive on goals or claim that they can perform more work than they are capable of accomplishing will be evident to an AI tool. While this may seem invasive to a person's privacy, that concern is set aside in favor of the ultimate goal, which is to maximize productivity.

MAKE GOOD DECISIONS

An employer wants to make good decisions regarding their employees. Using data collected, an organization can categorize the level of productivity and ranking of each employee. AI-based analysis is used to predict which of these employees will provide ongoing productivity. Decisions can then be made regarding these employees, and they can receive more training and be given increased responsibility.

Other employees might be productive only for a limited period of time, so they can be employed and then removed when they are no longer useful. Some employees need to be replaced or moved to a different role. The AI tools will manage a work environment similar to the way a sports coach looks at optimizing results and planning for the future. This analysis includes who is valuable and who needs to be replaced. The value of AI-based tools includes the ability to make predictions based on an employee's performance and personality, comparing that employee to a vast number of similar employees.

Also, the personal profile helps determine which job positions are most suitable for each employee. This might seem like stereotyping an employee, but it is really about making the organization as productive as possible. With AI technology, employees can be placed in job positions where they can contribute the most, and where their skills and competencies are well matched to the tasks assigned. Rather than having managers who are unsure or indecisive about work assignments, AI tools can make the decisions for them. Matching an employee to a role they are equipped to accomplish can quickly yield an increase in productivity and build trust between the manager and the employee.

IMPROVE EMPLOYEE MORALE

Good employee morale is a common goal for most organizations. The theory is that when employees are happy, there are usually higher rates of productivity. To determine an employee's morale, AI tools can collect and analyze data through natural language processing (NI P) Each individual employee can be monitored with their visual, verbal, and written clues all playing a part in their overall score. When an employee's morale declines, the AI software will trigger an analysis of their personality characteristics and determine the optimal method to return their morale to a higher level. If the employee is not particularly productive and the organization wants to terminate their employment, the employer can take action to fire the employee. By eliminating negative attitudes on an individual basis, the organization increases their allegiance to achieving its goals. It is also possible that no action is taken, and the employee can make the decision to leave the organization on their own accord.

Sentiment analysis using NLP has even more benefits. It can validate certain styles of communication as more or less effective, depending on the personality of the employee. It can also determine positive and negative trends across the various employee groups, and it can be used to compare results and trends across the organization. Rather than waiting until an employee's unhappiness spills into their work productivity, this provides a way for a manager to take proactive action.

IMPROVE COMMUNICATIONS

Using a psychological profile, a manager knows exactly how to interact with employees. The AI-based tools are capable of building a personality profile and determining effective messaging in a way that is highly persuasive. The manager has the ability to select the absolute best and most effective words of encouragement when motivating an employee or responding to an issue. With AI tools employed, the manager also has the ability to predict the person's reaction. Motivational messages can be delivered on an individual basis that resonate deeply and effectively with each employee. Employee responses are captured and added as new data to the individual's profile. This becomes an ongoing process for improving the AI-based tools.

Typically, when communicating with an employee, the message will start with a phrase to grab their attention and continue with content that is presented in a way that has the best possibility to connect with a receptive part of a person's mind. Based on historical personal data, an AI program will excel at communication. An additional benefit of AI-supported communication is the ability to modify communication based on language and culture. Today's workplace is a multicultural environment, and more organizations have a global workforce. This requires effective communication between local employees and those in different countries, and expressions between employees can easily be misinterpreted. Instead of employers becoming experts in understanding a culture, AI-based tools can help employers communicate effectively in a way that transcends cultural boundaries. AI may not always get the many nuances and humor in a language; however, it can translate words that are written and spoken as well as interpret the meaning behind the message. This opens doors to hire more people located around the world and find ways to make them productive. It also means that the organization can more easily replace its employees with less expensive workers, a significant cost-savings option. AI also allows for more effective communication with a customer who may not be familiar with the main language of the organization.

When I was managing a large staff, the easiest performance feedback was for high-performing employees. "Great work," I would say sincerely, or "Keep it up." How easy is that? The feedback for poorly performing employees took years to master and was never pleasant. I had to control my emotions and ask them details about their poor performance. The feedback had to be based on facts, and everything was documented. The language used was precise and important because it was scrutinized carefully by the employee for clues as to what was going to happen next. Poor language could also be used to launch grievances or turn into lawsuits if the employee was terminated. With AI, this can now be a structured script that a manager delivers. It will be precise, factual, and irrefutable.

The feedback discussions in which I felt the most useless were with the middle-performing group of employees. Their contribution was valuable, and to me they were the most dependable workers. High-performing employees had such a high level of motivation and work ethic that they were self-driven to be successful. The middle group were the workers who gave their best effort on a daily basis and were rewarded with a paycheck. What can be said other than, "Thank you"? With AI-based tools, the script can now be dedicated to making the middle group feel better and feel wanted. Feedback can be used to motivate them to higher levels of productivity. In this new AI-based environment, providing feedback and maintaining processes to keep them at this level becomes easier and more effective.

Video cameras are becoming increasingly popular, not only as security devices, but they are used by retailers and mall owners to track shopper buying preferences and their emotions.[20] These can track and measure customer shopping behavior through software such as location analytics and facial recognition. Cameras are also used in the workplace to assess the attitudes and motivations of each employee. Not everyone is good at recognizing visual cues that help identify a person's emotions. However, video combined with AI-based algorithms can easily help determine these cues.[21] Managers do not have the capability to analyze and evaluate personal characteristics and emotional state to the level of AI technology. Someone may say that a good manager would recognize when a person is upset or not feeling well. Remember, too, that the cameras are always present when the boss or manager isn't looking, so they would have a more accurate portrayal of the employee's psychological profile and emotional state overall. AI helps managers to customize their communication in the most effective way.

MAINTAIN A GOOD CORPORATE IMAGE

Employees provide value outside of workplace activities by continuing to promote a good image of the organization. This can create a positive brand image and increase the number of customers as well as the attractiveness for potential new employees. Using AI data collection methods, especially from social media, the organization can build a profile of how each employee represents the employer outside of the workplace. If the employee makes no reference to the organization, this is a neutral sentiment. However, any negative sentiment is quickly assessed, and appropriate action can be taken. AI-based profiling helps

20   Sarah Rieger, "At Least Two Malls Are Using Facial Recognition Technology to Track Shoppers' Ages and Genders without Telling," CBC News (CBC/Radio Canada, July 27, 2018), https://www.cbc.ca/news/canada/calgary/calgary-malls-1.4760964.
21   Affectiva, "Home," Affectiva, 2020, https://www.affectiva.com/.

to understand why the employee has this sentiment, and, based on the probability of success for each approach recommended, it can also recommend a corrective action.

In addition to employees, an organization can identify key stakeholders who work with the organization or have some association, such as suppliers, contractors, or a board of directors. AI-based tools can track their support or negative feelings. Similar to employees, AI tools can track these stakeholders outside the workplace based on verbal or written communication. Using their communication and emotional state, NLP can assess the satisfaction, stress, and frustration these stakeholders might have and whether it relates to their perception of the organization. Rather than wait for problems that might proliferate and damage the organization's image or reputation, action can be taken to resolve any negative sentiment. It is an opportunity to act quickly as opposed to waiting for worsening conditions. Corrective action can be taken that resonates with the individual, or alternate action can be taken to sever the relationship. This is another opportunity when AI-based tools provide an advantage.

SUMMARY

While the actions and decisions taken with regard to employee performance using AI-based tools might seem overbearing and even harsh, the expected result is a highly capable group of employees who work together well. As part of the employment relationship, employees agree to the terms and conditions of their responsibilities, which now include employee data being collected and used by the organization. Productivity can be addressed on a customized basis and include well-defined actions on job promotions and terminations. Communication will dramatically improve as each employee receives a message that resonates with their personal goals.

The expectation is that most employees will be satisfied as the morale of workers and image of the organization are optimized, while the number of AI tools employed within their organization is ignored. The outcome is an environment where an organization easily achieves higher productivity, as well as other objectives it sets for all employees. The work environment becomes one where employees are influenced with such great effectiveness that they believe they are self-motivated toward their own goals. Employees are vulnerable and become susceptible to the power of psychological influence. However, before employees are ready to defend themselves, there needs to be a basic understanding of the mechanics of how the tools work, and that is revealed in the next chapter.

CHAPTER 5

The Magic behind AI Programs

It is important to understand some of the technical aspects so that employees can develop effective strategies to retaliate against software that is trying to build a perfect psychological profile. AI programs do not perform magic. They use software programming to produce results. The two most common components used by artificial intelligence developers are machine learning and natural language processing. Machine learning is a software program that uses data to create a model and then uses that model to perform prediction or classification. Essentially, the computer algorithm learns from data over time and then tries to determine a rule or procedure that can predict future data. Prediction is a powerful capability because it is a way to entice us to make purchases or manage our behavior in the workplace. Machine learning is also a critical component responsible for the evolution of self-driving vehicles in which the navigation and driver-behavior patterns become predicted events. Machine learning is responsible for developments such as facial recognition and the interpretation of emotions based on facial expression. NLP is a computer program's ability to interpret human language and classify the communication or create a response. This is accomplished by breaking down the language and interpreting the words and phrases to determine an intent. This is the software that enables commonly used virtual assistants such as Siri, Alexa, or Google Assistant.

Machine learning algorithms use our personal data as input and build a profile that is essentially a replica of who we are. It can predict how we will react to any variety of specific communications. The profile is an important tool that, when combined with psychological models, can be used to influence our decisions. It is more obvious in the marketing world when we click on a book to purchase from Amazon or buy something based on a Google ad. This technology is being adopted by organizations to increase productivity in the workforce. It is important to learn how this technology works before it gains complete access to our data and builds a psychological profile that can predict our thoughts and actions.

HOW MACHINE LEARNING WORKS

A machine learning algorithm is software code written in a programming language, which is a set vocabulary and rules for instructing a computer to perform certain tasks. Some examples of programming languages that can be used to create a machine learning program are Python, R, and Java. The program contains mathematic equations that use the data to build a sample of what the data represents. To create a personal profile, all your data is fed into the machine learning algorithm, and the result is a model that represents you. Machine learning programs use different methods to create decision-making algorithms, the most recognizable one being a neural network. Neural networks are software code that was inspired by the human brain; there are nodes that provide the functions of input, analysis, and output. Machine "learning" occurs in a number of ways, but the most common are as follows.

Unsupervised learning occurs when the data is not labeled, but with a sufficient number of clues, the algorithm will be able to classify the data effectively. If the data indicates that an object has leaves, a trunk, and branches, then the algorithm will correctly classify it as a tree. The main benefit of unsupervised learning is clustering. The algorithm simply groups similar items together. This is frequently used in something known as a recommender system, where if you like a certain book or movie, the algorithm looks at similar books or movies and recommends that you purchase them.

Supervised learning occurs when the input data is already labeled. The algorithm is trained to correlate any new data with the already labeled dataset. The algorithm is capable of modifying the model until it obtains the most accurate correlation. It is then used on test data to verify the accuracy of the model. Supervised learning is used in health care to diagnose x-ray results, for example. The algorithm is trained on numerous x-ray images, labeled as either healthy or showing evidence of a condition, and is then used on a new, unique pattern to make a diagnosis of the condition. Supervised learning used in this field provides higher accuracy than a trained technician.[22]

Reinforcement learning occurs when the algorithm learns through trial and error to make proper predictions. A common example is when you type on a smartphone and the full word appears after only two or three letters. You may type in a word or a name, and it recommends a

---

22   Hanae Armitage, "X-ray Results Can Provide Higher Accuracy than a Trained Technician," Medical Xpress, November, 2018, https://medicalxpress.com/news/2018-11-ai-outperformed-radiologists-screening-x-rays.html.

different name entirely. Eventually, after you delete the word multiple times, the phone learns your patterns and learns that it is not the word you want. This happened with a business name, "Stonemeadow," which is a word not found in a dictionary. At first, the smartphone ignored the recommendation and typed in the name correctly. On the second try, it again recommended other words, but by the third attempt, the smartphone learned that the most likely word was "Stonemeadow," and now it correctly recommends that name every time.

UNDERSTANDING CORRELATION

Creating an accurate model, or personal profile, means finding the best fit in the data that is collected about each employee and matched to a specific psychological profile. The main mathematical process is known as regression analysis. In simple terms, this means finding the closest pattern that can represent a set of data, which is the main function of machine learning algorithms.

In order for AI to predict anything, it needs to have and analyze the correct data points. A simple way to explain this is to review a variety of graphs that can be used to plot the data. Something that should be familiar to those who took a statistics class is a normal distribution. This is also known as a bell-shaped curve and is shown in Figure 4. A normal distribution is used to represent values for a series of random events. One of the major concepts of this is that as you collect more random data, the distribution of the shape of the curve does not change. In the graph, there are two tails at the end of the distribution curve. If your data is closer to the middle of the bell curve, then an AI analysis will find it easier to understand and predict your behavior. Deceiving AI tools is about finding a way to provide more data that is statistically unusual, or closer to either tail in the distribution.

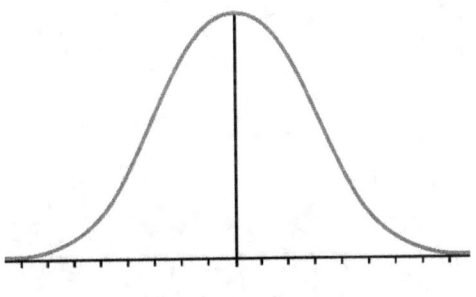

Figure 4:

To understand how to deceive a machine learning algorithm, there needs to be an explanation of how regression is used to represent correlations in the data. The simplest form of regression is called linear regression and is a statistical method to understand the relationship between two variables, or data points. In Figure 5, each data point is plotted on the graph. Using linear regression, which is a mathematical equation, a line can be drawn to show the closest correlation to the dataset. The line in Figure 6 shows how the dataset is correlated. For AI to complete an analysis, there have to be many valid data points to determine a correlation.

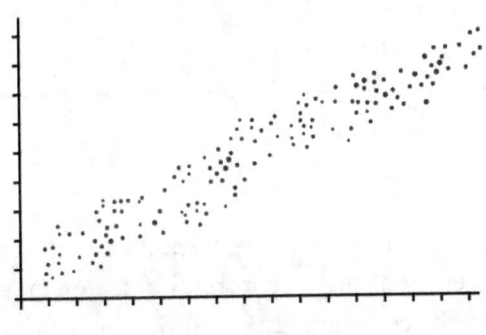

Figure 5

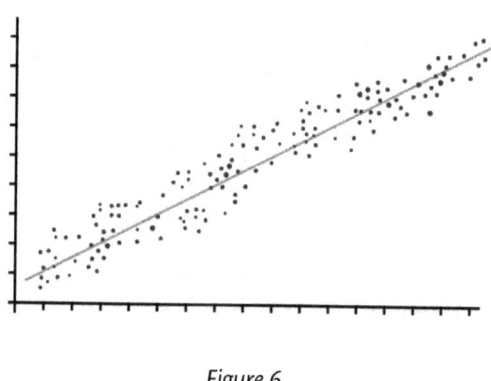

Figure 6

In Figure 7, the data points do not show a positive correlation, and therefore it is less likely to be able to make an accurate prediction when given a new data point. Understanding this type of pattern is the starting point that is needed to deceive a machine learning algorithm.

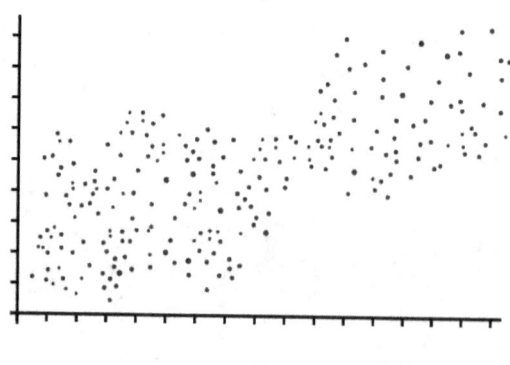

Figure 7

Logistic regression is the main concept used in creating neural networks. The accuracy of the correlation is based on creating a line or curve based on the correlation that best fits the data. In Figure 8, the curve is the best representation of the data and can be used to predict that a new data point will fall on or close to the curve.

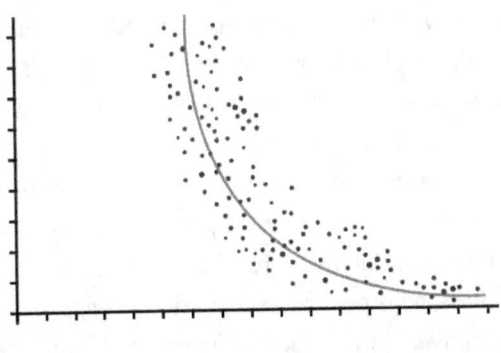

Figure 8

This is a simplified introduction to statistics and regression and should provide enough conceptual information needed to build a strategy to resist. The concepts will be applied to create ways to confuse the AI-based algorithms.

HOW NLP WORKS

NLP interprets human language and classifies communication into a meaning or, as it is called in NLP, an "intent." Software uses similarity between words and phrases to determine what you are asking. When we ask Siri to tell a joke, Siri analyzes the content of our communication and identifies our intent. NLP is also used to search documents or text such as emails and text messages to extract meaning as well as determine correlations and anomalies. For example, NLP can assess recently sent emails and text messages to determine your level of satisfaction with your work. NLP can also analyze your current mood and predict the probability that you will miss a deadline. The purpose of these tools is to help the organization find a way to increase or maximize productivity. After all, resources are frequently the most expensive cost for an organization.

Another ability of NLP is interpreting emotion based on the words or phrases used, which is known as sentiment analysis. This is a very interesting concept because we all use words differently and have different backgrounds. NLP performs sentiment analysis when an employee creates a communication, such as an email, and the words are compared to what is known as a *corpus*. A corpus is a large body of language samples, containing words and phrases that help determine whether the message is positive or negative. Words such as "like" and "happy" are positive. Phrases such as "good work" and "helpful contribution" are positive. Words such as "annoyed" and "angry" are negative. In any organization, there are certain common phrases used for specific work, which can also be used in the interpretation of sentiment. This normally requires creating or obtaining a corpus, a body of work that is relevant to the work environment where the sentiment analysis is being performed. Most workplaces have unique language and jargon that can be misinterpreted by NLP unless there is a reference document.

The purpose of analysis is to collect workplace messages, known as utterances, and compare the language used to the corpus to determine intent and sentiment. A common expression such as, "We are working on the second iteration" might be considered good or a bad depending on the context. "I need to start over because I reconsidered the design plan" might be interpreted as negative, although it could indicate a commitment to quality, which is positive. There needs to be a clear vocabulary and common phrase documentation for the work environment for NLP to properly understand the intent and determine the sentiment correctly.

NLP is a very important AI tool, is fairly straightforward to implement, and can be used for incredible benefit. NLP was used to help children under the age of eight who were unable to properly express emotional suffering. Before AI, it was solely the responsibility of adults to recognize their child's problems and seek treatment. Recently developed AI tools can now detect depression based on the child's speech, and with early diagnosis, the children respond well to treatment.[23] A voice analysis software program has also been developed that understands human speech and is capable of detecting post-traumatic stress disorder (PTSD).[24] The algorithm is trained to listen for minor variables and auditory markers that are imperceptible to the human ear. The algorithm can diagnose PTSD with 89 percent accuracy.

Based on a person's voice, AI-based tools using NLP can also detect mental illness and possibly other medical conditions. If a person slurs their speech during a stressful meeting, are they having a stroke? The potential for sentiment analysis goes significantly beyond positive or negative feelings. Voice analysis tools will be able to identify when someone is nervous about being able to achieve the end date for a task but does not want to reveal any problems. People who are overly aggressive on goals or claim they can perform more work than they are capable of performing will be evident to an AI tool. While this may seem invasive to a person's privacy, the goal is to increase productivity. There are many workshops, courses, and published research documents on how a manager needs to improve interactions with people, and now NLP combined with machine learning software promises to provide a more accurate solution in real time. Is there a difference if a well-trained manager detects a problem in a person's commitments or well-being, versus a machine learning tool that identifies the same condition?

Now that machines can analyze and identify our behavior, and uncover our personalities, these algorithms can have a dramatic influence on how humans interact with machines. NLP-based algorithms can be used to extract personality and behavioral traits and integrate these

---

23   University of Vermont, "AI Can Detect Depression in a Child's Speech," Science Daily, May 6, 2019, https://www.sciencedaily.com/releases/2019/05/190506150126.htm.

24   Dave Philipps, "The Military Wants Better Tests for PTSD. Speech Analysis Could Be the Answer," The New York Times Magazine, April 19, 2019, https://www.nytimes.com/2019/04/22/magazine/veterans-ptsd-speech-analysis.html.

into a person's work profile. This program is a significant achievement for an employer because it can build a complete psychological profile that is used as the basis to find the most effective way to communicate with an employee.

HOW AI BUILDS A PROFILE

Data is the nourishment that feeds AI tools. It may not be obvious, but a lot of data is easily gathered about employee activities. As previously mentioned, work activity is tracked by software applications, and any completed work is captured. Communication to coworkers by email, text, or a workflow tool is detected. Video cameras capture images and track movement. Video capture can also be used to determine moods or feelings based on facial expression. Microphones pick up voice communication. This might be from a conferencing tool such as Skype or Zoom. If the organization places microphones around the workplace, then any verbal expression can be captured. Your location can be tracked from your smartphone. All of this data is collected and used by a machine learning algorithm to create a profile.

Typically, raw data is classified or categorized before being used. For example, NLP captures you saying, "Has that been decided?" Meanwhile, it captures your colleague responding with, "Let's make a list of what we need to do." NLP categorizes these expressions into different personality types. If you are familiar with the Myers-Briggs Type Indicator of personality, NLP will classify your expression into "perceiving," which generally is a person who keeps things open-ended and is flexible. It would categorize your colleague's response as "judging," or generally someone who wants matters to be settled and structured. These behaviors and styles of communication are all data points that can be fed to the program to determine your psychological profile. AI tools use the input data to create a model that represents your personality, and this is compared to a variety of personality types to determine the best match. Your personality type combined with an interpretation of your emotions allows the software to determine your psychological profile.

A machine learning algorithm consists of equations that perform regression analysis to correlate your data into a model as well to compare it to other models. The process is to load the data, validate that the data has an acceptable structure, and ensure the datasets are labeled. The algorithm executes to create a correlation in the data, and this becomes the model. The program itself is fairly simple. There are a number of factors known as hyperparameters, such as the number of iterations performed in the programming analysis, that need to be predetermined, but studies have shown that it is input data that has the greatest impact on the results. A greater volume of data results in building a better model. The labels for the datasets need to be accurate, and for supervised learning, the labels should be balanced, which means a reasonable number of each label.

There are typically two major problems with data when building a personal profile: insufficient data and outliers. Insufficient data causes the model to be less accurate and therefore less reliable. Providing less data about yourself in the workplace is one way to reduce the accuracy of the profile. However, this is not a guarantee that a deficit model won't be used anyway. An inaccurate model is less reliable, but it might result in a worse experience for workplace interactions. The second issue with data is managing outliers. An outlier is an event or piece of data that does not fit well. For example, let's say that all of the results for a test are between 70 and 90 percent, but there is one result of 25 percent. What can be predicted about the results for someone new taking the test? Similarly, if you see a flock of sparrows and one falcon, how do you represent the results? Machine learning algorithms normally ignore the outlier, and this creates a problem if more outliers become evident. For a personal profile, outliers help distract an algorithm from creating an accurate model and can be used in the strategy for resistance.

The model becomes your personal profile and is used to drive you to be more productive as well as to perform what the organization wants you to do, whether you feel like it or not. Have you met a person who was so charismatic that you wanted to listen and follow what they said? This is similar to what a model creates. It taps into your personality and finds the best way to communicate a thought that you will have no ability to resist. When you walk up to a person who has an object in their hand, and they put their hand out with the object in, it is human nature to reach our hand out to accept it. AI takes advantage of human nature.

As AI algorithms are introduced and start to assess data, they are likely to have a lower probability of creating a good match based on employee profiles. It takes time to get the right data and make sure it is giving good results. This is especially true if the data is for a new employee compared to data that has been collected on a person who has worked in the organization for a few years. The greatest weakness of AI is a lack of data or messy data. In AI language, the lack of data results in inaccurate models, which is referred to as *underfitting*. Underfitting means that there is insufficient data to create a reliable model. There is a danger, however, that an organization might attempt to use the data anyway, and the outcomes are not predictable. Using a poor model can result in the opposite of what is trying to be accomplished.

Once sufficiently large amounts of data are collected, the next step is to ensure that it is structured in order for machine learning tools to access it. *Structured data* means the data is organized, easily accessible, and in a common format. Of course, this should be defined before collection begins, but there will always be a need to validate the data once it is in a database. The structured data is fed into the software program that contains the machine learning algorithms.

It is unlikely that an employer will know about the total amount of data that is collected on its employees. Data collection about work activities can be performed by vendor software programs based on a series of predefined fields and triggers. External data collection is performed by web scrapers that grab anything associated with you. Think about your workday, your tasks accomplished, and all the times you use the internet. These are all measurable data points and can become part of the development strategy we can use to defend ourselves. Personal profile models use analyzed data as the basis for the organization to act or deliver a personalized message. The collection of data and the importance of data are two critical factors that will help us create our strategy to reduce the accuracy and reliability of these tools.

SUMMARY

Machine learning and natural language processing are two common tools used for AI applications. It's not magic. This is code written in a programming language such as Python, and it uses mathematical equations to find correlations in data. The correlations are used to develop in-depth knowledge about an employee. A typical machine learning program uses a neural network to optimize data correlations. Learning takes place based on labels that support supervised learning. NLP analyzes text and extracts more data from employee communication that is fed to AI programs. Understanding some of the technical aspects is important so we can learn the best ways to retaliate against software that is trying to build a perfect psychological profile.

This section began to identify some factors that can impede the creation of accurate results when performing regression analysis. A lack of sufficient data, data outliers, and a series of datasets that have a problem with labels all contribute to poor results. This knowledge will help us when we consider our plan to deceive AI tools. The mathematics for machine learning is complicated and require interpretation to make the results more accurate. While vendors or program creators might suggest the results are meaningful, a greater understanding of statistics and statistical error might suggest otherwise. A deeper explanation of the math behind the tools is described later, but first we need to define some effective techniques to plan the deception.

CHAPTER 6

How to Deceive AI Tools

I f you are employed by an organization and under constant scrutiny by AI tools, there are ways to hide your personal information, confuse the algorithms with misleading data points, and enhance your profile by supplying suitable data. Perhaps this chapter should be titled "How to *Deliberately* Deceive AI Tools" since the content is an employee's guide to deceiving the algorithms. The algorithms create a personal profile with an intent to manipulate your behavior. That profile is used by an organization to influence you in a customized way. The plan for deceiving machine learning algorithms is to make it difficult to distinguish between real and fake data about ourselves, similar to how it can be difficult to determine real news from fake news on the internet. This confusion can result in the fake data being accepted or the real data being rejected.

Dating websites are a good example of manipulating a personal profile and people using photos to fool a matching algorithm. The dating app suggests potential matches based on these embellishments.

Some profiles are known to contain fake photos and even false, or at least exaggerated, personal information. In the workplace, there are also people who try to enhance their status in the organization by taking credit for another person's work, constantly highlighting their accomplishments, regardless of who is listening, and positioning themselves as the model employee. Some of this will become more difficult with AI technology watching and collecting data. On the other hand, this type of deception has some valuable tips for employees trying to deceive surveillance and AI-based manipulation in the workplace.

DECEPTION STRATEGIES

There are three main strategies to deceive machine learning algorithms. The first relies on limiting the data provided, and the second is to provide outliers, meaning data points that are unusual or break a pattern. Both methods are an attempt to reduce the reliability of the machine learning results. A profile that has a low reliability score means that the organization is limited in their confidence to manipulate you and also limited in the ability to provide negative criticism of your work effort. The third way to deceive AI is to deliberately supply data points that inadvertently build an amazing profile of you as an employee, which helps promote your capability and advancement in the organization. Some of the tactics used to implement these strategies will overlap. That is advantageous because we want the machine learning model to reflect our personal objectives and not those created by a software program.

Table 3: Deception Strategies

Strategy	Impact
Limit the amount of data collection	Insufficient data for model creation
Provide outliers	Model reliability is reduced
Supply personally desired data points	Model reflects ideal profile instead of a realistic profile

There is a difference between simple employee monitoring to improve performance and taking it a step further by using AI-based tools. Taking action in a work environment based on monitoring employee behaviors is a long-standing tradition for employers. The advantages of AI tools are the ability to create a psychological profile and then the use of that profile to persuade and motivate an employee much more easily and with far greater effectiveness. The industry or type of work is less important because the data collection is personal, not industry related. The personal models are customized to individuals, and actions taken are grounded in psychology, not the work environment. AI is flexible about how data is collected, as long as there is sufficient data to be used by machine learning algorithms.

AI tools have the ability to combine a deep understanding of personality traits with motivational theories to create a powerful influence on an employee. If all of this is a bit intimidating, it may be easier to take it one step at a time. Once you understand what motivates you, you have a greater understanding as to how a tool could manipulate you based on your personality. You can start by knowing a bit more about yourself. Try to acquire some knowledge on personality traits by reading some books or articles, and perhaps take a Myers-Briggs test. Then review a few of the most popular motivational theories and compare this to where you might fit. By knowing your personality type, you not only get a better understanding of your strengths and weaknesses, but also how you make decisions and confront emotions. With a little training, you can understand what makes you happy and what is most likely to motivate you. With practice you will become faster at recognizing what motivates you and others around you.

The most dangerous aspect of personality profiling and analysis is when the tools use facial and verbal expressions to build a psychological profile that will subsequently be used to determine an appropriate communication. Our moods change from day to day and even during a day. Although it may be difficult for some, we need to learn to manage our communication and how we unknowingly use our body language to express our feelings. We need to think before we speak and be aware that what we say is being intensely analyzed. To provide a poor correlation, we need to smile at appropriate times, then grimace at strange times.

This can be explained by referring to a couple of very old books. The first, *The One Minute Manager*, describes techniques for goal setting, praising, and reprimanding employees.[25] It is a guide for how managers can be very efficient and offers tips on how to delegate tasks successfully. My preference is the counterposition, a book called *The 59-Second Employee*.[26] The title refers to being one second ahead of the manager's methods. It describes how to recognize and counteract the standard techniques used by the one-minute manager. It is a great example of how employees can "manage up." Several of the techniques apply to how AI will try to manage employees using machine learning algorithms. The goal is to be one step ahead and manage the data provided so that the organization does not have a sufficiently reliable tool to force you into conformity or imprison you in a data algorithm.

---

25 Ken Blanchard, Spencer Johnson, *The One-Minute Manager*, Willian Morrow & Co., 1982.

26 Dr. Rae Andre, Peter Ward, *The 59-Second Employee*, HarperCollins, 1984.

SUMMARY

This chapter identifies three main strategies for deceiving AI tools and taking back control of your work life. However, the first step is to learn more about yourself. AI-based tools will connect with standard psychological profiles, and you need to have some level of understanding of where you fit so that you can resist and retaliate against being permanently profiled. The easiest way to control the profile being created is to control the input, which is the data that is collected. AI tools are constantly determining the best way to classify each new piece of data or a complete dataset, and the data must be compared to existing research models. In many situations, we can determine what data we want to provide. The objective is to stay ahead of the algorithms by managing the data that they use for input. It is a straightforward approach that has the best chance of successfully disrupting the accuracy and reliability of the results produced by the AI software. The next chapter starts the review of ways for you to take control.

CHAPTER 7

Deception Strategy: Limit the Amount of Data

The most obvious place to limit data collection is in the workplace. That is where most of the software-tracking tools are deployed and where the personal profiles are created. An employer may use vendor software to collect and analyze or create their own data collection and model creation software programs. In the workplace, we normally provide data in two ways: working on our assigned tasks and spending time away from our assigned tasks. Performing some creative thinking or problem-solving in a quiet space is not something that can be collected as a positive data point.

A difficult area to reduce personal data points is while completing assigned activities. Organizations typically monitor progress and include completed activities in the process of collecting organizational metrics. If you understand the metrics being collected, you can manage your data points appropriately. For example, you can complete tasks on time but ignore quality issues if those are not being monitored and reported. Aside from the obvious performance metrics, a machine learning program uses additional data to create a personal profile, and this is where you can be careful with the data you provide.

An obvious solution might be to prevent the surveillance altogether. There is software where you can set your status to permanently active.[27] Consequently, employers request that vendors prevent any blocking capability by employees. Providing no data can be a dangerous strategy, so allowing a limited amount of data is a better choice.

COMMUNICATION

Reducing the number of data points includes minimizing the amount of communication. This may seem rather impossible at first, given our tech-savvy work environments. However, there are steps we can take to easily reduce the number of data points. Emails need to be specific to a purpose and related to one of your objectives and should never include personal judgments. In fact, you should learn to identify and use neutral words as much as possible. The same is true for other communication, such as text messages and even verbal communication. Use neutral words and avoid making judgments such as "bad" and "terrible." Rather than sending an email that reports your task is late or incomplete, you can list the due date and the current forecast of when it will be complete and let that indicate the status. It might still reflect on your work-performance metrics, but at least it won't be included in sentiment analysis. Similarly, when speaking to other employees, use neutral words and especially avoid overly descriptive words.

---

27 Alex Christian, *Bosses Started Spying on Remote Workers. Now They're Fighting Back*, Wired, August 10, 2020. https://www.wired.co.uk/article/work-from-home-surveillance-software.

Table 4: Examples of Neutral Phrases

Phrases to avoid	Try this
I hate this place.	My current workplace is different than I expected.
The boss is an idiot.	Our manager makes decisions that are difficult to understand.
The work assigned to me is boring, and I cannot wait for the day to end.	My work is not aligned with the achievement of my personal goals.

No one really talks like the suggestions in the second column of table 4, but the point is to reduce the number of descriptive words that can be classified as negative sentiment. Unhappy words can be used to identify employees who have a bad attitude by a machine learning algorithm using NLP. We like to use colorful adjectives, especially when we get emotional, but that is the most important time to use neutral words. Emotion-laden words can accumulate and turn what might be a one-time outburst into a more serious amount of collected negative sentiment.

There is also a need to understand the work culture to truly find a way to fit in and express the words that the organization wants to hear. A younger culture may prefer to hear terms such as "exciting" and "innovative," while an older, more conservative workplace might be more amenable to phrases such as "wanting to reduce risk," "adhere to standards," and "follow policy."

Perhaps the language used by the organization is not your native language. There is a great opportunity to deceive NLP with a heavy accent, as well as expressions in your language that do not translate well. It may be suspicious if you have a much heavier accent when speaking about work issues than you use when speaking casually with coworkers, so care must be taken if this is part of your strategy. However, if you have another colleague who speaks the same language and is also concerned about AI, you could have more of your meetings in your native language. You can add in slang or local expressions to increase the chance of the communications being misinterpreted. Also, body language tends to be different in different cultures, although a well-trained, more expensive AI program might be able to decipher this. If your organization decides to implement a cheaper version of surveillance software, it might not be able to understand anything that you do or say. Every situation is different.

NLP also has difficulty understanding sarcasm. You can say anything with positive words and then put the emphasis at a certain place in a sentence and it changes the meaning. This is a great way to confuse AI. You can say, "This is a great organization," and NLP thinks it is positive. You can say the same phrase and, emphasizing the first word, turn the sentence into a question, and NLP will have trouble understanding the true meaning. At some point in the future, that may change; however, in the meantime it's a great way to confuse AI. Depending on the quality of the NLP analysis and database used to train it, there are a few more suggestions that may work. Using slang might fool an AI tool. Using another language or mixing words from two languages in a communication might also be effective. One very important item to remember is that emojis do not fool NLP. The software can be configured easily to interpret both emojis and emoticons created from a keyboard. Finally, NLP might not be aware of certain expressions that are disparaging, such as this project is "in the gutter," or this work is "brutal."

IMAGES

If the workplace has video cameras, the same principle applies to facial expression and body language. To deceive AI tools, you need to express less emotion. This becomes a difficult task because a blank expression can also be interpreted as someone who is depressed. It is better to minimize emotions in facial and body language in specific situations. These include meetings with a direct supervisor, listening to senior staff, or when you are assigned a type of work that you do not enjoy. Perhaps you can nod your head in agreement while hiding your true feelings of disgust. This is the type of body language and verbal expression that confuses AI-based tools. You can cross your arms in front of you, take an aggressive stance leaning forward and say, "I think that idea is great," and the AI tools will have opposing signals to interpret.

We must be more vigilant when there is a potential for video capture. For example, when you are in a meeting and a manager is speaking, you can smile and appear receptive. You must be in control of the image that is presented. Don't laugh or snicker at a poorly presented PowerPoint slide. Don't doodle, or the cameras might capture a data point that suggests a lack of attention. It will not be easy to constantly be on guard, and it is not necessary. You simply need to provide fewer data points—and especially data points that are negative.

One way to fool AI image analysis is to smile a lot, even though you are not happy. Smiling reflects positivity. When meeting people for the first time, it will be important to smile and be friendly so that they have a good impression of you, and AI will think that you have good interpersonal skills. Perhaps you should tell a joke and make them laugh. Deceiving the facial expression analysis tools will be difficult, although anyone who had Botox injections in their forehead or lips will be more difficult to read. Botox tends to reduce the ability to move the muscles, which reduces the ability to accurately read facial expression. It will also be important to limit hand gestures when speaking in case the analysis tools incorporate that movement into the data. For example, finger-pointing can be interpreted as aggressive behavior, which is not a good workplace trait.

EXTERNAL COMMUNICATION

The greatest opportunity to limit data is to stop or hide all personal communication that is not work-related. This may be difficult for some, but be aware that any time you use an organization's network or hardware, they have the ability to track and collect the contents of everything you create. Using a personal email account to send an email over the organization's network does not ensure privacy. All email can be intercepted and inspected based on the premise that the organization is checking for malware.

There are ways to send encrypted emails by using Gmail or through other email providers; however, technology changes so quickly that you need to search for a current provider of encrypted email for personal use and try it. Even with this plan, encrypted emails on the organization's network will be flagged and can be traced to originate back to you. If you send email using your personal smartphone, then be sure that you are not using the organization's Wi-Fi network, or once again they will have access to the content. Is it safe to use your personal phone to send emails to friends without the organization having any access? It is possible, but this issue will be discussed further in a later section. If your plan is to use free or open source encrypted email, that might not be the best solution. Free email is frequently tied to advertising. If you send an email that includes contents about going on vacation, don't be surprised when you start seeing targeted ads for vacation destinations.

If you must surf the internet for personal use while at work, use a private browsing feature on your browser. A private browser prevents web browsers from recording your history. The intent is to prevent cookies from capturing data about you and building a profile in the way that normal browsers do now in order to find something to sell you, or at the very least, something for you to click on. A more secure option is to use software that allows you to browse anonymously, such as Tor. Once it is configured, third party trackers are unable to follow you, and cookies are deleted when the browsing session ends.

This type of solution takes you to a separate network where monitoring is not possible and traffic is encrypted. Another item to consider is to encrypt any personal files that you store on a work computer. There are several software programs that make this possible. Another good strategy is to mistype important words, use symbols to represent words, and avoid being concise and clear in written or verbal communication. Use as many neutral words as possible. This is the opposite of good business communication practice, which might become a little confusing for your manager. However, the game is to fool or trick the machine learning algorithm in a way that it is unable to determine your personality and sentiment.

Table 5: Examples of Limiting Data Collection

Personal profile data source	Action	Impact on machine learning
Work activities	• Complete assignments on time, regardless of quality or scope • Defer or reassign complex activities to others so machine learning tools do not pick up any negative data points • Schedule leave or sick days at critical times when you want to avoid providing negative data points	Minimizes the number of negative data points
Work communication	• Only communicate when required • Be brief and use neutral words	Minimizes valid data points

Workplace image	• Arrive and leave at inconsistent times • Smile at people and use neutral words	Provides common data that is useless for creating a unique profile
Social media profile	• Create a fake professional profile and use intermittently • Create two separate social media profiles	Ensures insufficient data is obtained
Extracurricular activities	• Use a different version of your personal profile accounts • Avoid or restrict any media coverage of any kind	Reduces data gathered by web scraping

When communicating, the language content needs to be neutral rather than emotional in case the sentiment analysis tool mistakes personal expressions to mean something bad. Refrain from sending personal emails or texts from a workplace email address. If possible, log in with a different account to send personal messages. This also applies to social media since organizations have become more interested in employee monitoring. The answer is to have two accounts. One account will be a profile that shows you very favorably: beautiful photo, sensible blogs, relevant likes, and connections to the most impressive people in your field. Meanwhile, you have a second account that you can use to perform all your regular interactions and not worry about being traced, because it does not appear to be attached to you as an employee. Use one account to conduct your work activities, such as work-related purchases, and a different account to hide your bad habits.

When you are away from work due to illness or on vacation, be sure to completely disconnect from the workplace. This ensures that no updates are made to your profile. Sick leave and vacation time are not appropriate times for data collection. You need to protect your personal life and not allow collection software to monitor personal exceptions and include those data points in an attempt to control your work life.

SOCIAL MEDIA

Many organizations gather data about an employee's social media activities. Removing yourself or reducing interaction with social media can be difficult and requires you to be selective about the accounts you have online and the content you have in them. The first step is to review and delete as many personal online accounts and smartphone apps as possible. Even if you do not use the account, there is stored data, and the account probably links you to other services. The deactivation process can be frustrating, and there is probably no guarantee that the historical data will be removed. However, when you stop using an account, you prevent the creation of new data points about yourself. Also consider removing or limiting your personal email accounts, especially if you have more than one. This may sound strange, but most people have more than one email address. Commit to a main personal email address, and perhaps a backup, and then make sure there are no other email addresses that are traceable to you. Restricting data from social media activities is complex because many online sites are owned by one company. Google owns YouTube, and Facebook owns Instagram. While these are obvious examples, there are a lot more, and many online logins are linked. Often you will be asked to log in to a new site with an existing Gmail account.

Getting off social media completely is a radical step for most people. However, organizations collect external data about you all the time. In sports, personal activities are monitored to verify they conform to an expected code of conduct for professional athletes. For normal employees, it is difficult to believe that an employer can track you outside the workplace. Enter your name in a search engine and see how much is of your life is available online. This is all collected by data brokers who host sites that contain harvested data about people based on public records and social media. The brokers then offer it for sale to organizations. Therefore, you need to try to have your data removed from data broker sites, which is not always possible. It is fairly easy for data brokers to create code that performs a web search scouring the internet, finding a name, and capturing all available data regarding that name. This type of web search can be created using only about eight lines of programming code. Organizations pay money to a data broker for access to the data, thereby sidestepping the process of collecting it themselves. Finding data brokers might be easy, but getting them to remove your data could be more difficult. There is no magic solution to share because the steps and processes to remove yourself from a data broker's site undergo regular changes. However, one strategy is to create a profile with a lack of data, which creates a problem called underfitting, as discussed in chapter 5. The model cannot create a viable profile based on an insufficient amount of data.

To make browsing from outside your workplace more private, use a virtual private network (VPN) connection. This encrypts the data being sent back and forth and is used for remote workers to provide a secure connection to an organization's network. It is also available for ordinary consumers who purchase specific internet cybersecurity and antivirus software. One note about encryption is that is does not encrypt everything. Metadata is defined as data that describes other data, and metadata is not part of a normal encryption process. For example, the contents of an email can be encrypted, but the metadata will still show that you are the originator, the date and time the email was created, the date and time that it was sent, and the destination.

You need to create a separate social media profile that cannot be linked to your employment. One of the easiest ways to do this is to never use a recognizable photo of yourself. Instead, create an avatar for social media and any other site where it proves useful. I doubt that an AI image recognition app will be able to match your avatar to you. Your friends will also learn to recognize your avatar. An iPhone using facial recognition can be fooled into staying locked if you wear large sunglasses or a facemask, but your friends will still recognize you. You should also create a separate email address that you do not provide to anyone on the internet. Never provide your phone number online, and use a fake phone number if the site insists on one. Phone numbers have become our personal brand and are frequently the key data field for numerous applications. When I pick up my dry cleaning, they ask for my phone number. When I go to the pharmacy to refill a prescription, they ask for my phone number. When I want to dispute my electricity bill, they ask for my phone number. It is the single most marketable piece of data that connects you to everything else. You need to stop completing online surveys that ask for your email address and phone number. They are simply harvesting personal information to use or sell.

When you limit the amount of data collected, there is a possibility that the algorithm will have insufficient data to create a model. As stated previously, in machine learning language, this is known as underfitting. The software attempts to create a correlation based on too few data points, and this results in low reliability. The number of data points required might be based on a minimum standard set by the organization or based on the relative volume of data gathered for all employee profiles. Regardless, a lack of data results in a model that is less reliable as a predictor of your behavior.

SUMMARY

Limiting the amount of data that you provide sounds simple. It is a lot more difficult, however, when you realize the level of activity most people spend online and the number of data points being collected. Keystrokes, verbal communication, emails, and facial expressions are all available for collection as data points about you. In addition, your actions outside the workplace can also be monitored. You need to live your own life, so find a way to be yourself without having it connected to your work persona. The purpose of reducing data is to make the models less reliable. Follow the recommendations, and you will at least be ahead of others in the workplace.

CHAPTER 8

Deception Strategy: Provide Personal Outliers

Creating an outlier requires a break from normal habits. Let's say that all of your data points indicate that you're an introvert. They show that you enjoy reading a good book and that you take long walks by yourself. If you want the data to indicate you as more extroverted, then provide some different data points. An outlier may be having someone post a video of you dancing wildly at a party surrounded by screaming people. When I learn of someone who volunteers at elderly homes, chats with them, and takes them for a walk, I see a person who has empathy. An outlier for this empathetic person might be throwing recyclable material directly in the garbage or throwing it out the window of the car. In the workplace, creating an outlier means a change from normal habits. If you never speak in a meeting, take one meeting and be well prepared to talk and express all your thoughts. If you are always showing other workers how to complete a task, take time to ask someone else what you are supposed to do. This requires you to think about your habits and provide a data point that is different.

Confusing the AI tool means providing cues and data points that are false. This might mean holding your stomach, even if you do not feel sick. Or it could mean bouncing along with a spring in your step, even though you are exhausted. The purpose of misdirection is to give false images of both who you are and what to expect from your behaviors. With sufficient confusion, the AI tool results will either have a very low reliability or simply be unable to arrive at a meaningful correlation to a psychological profile. When the data points are scattered, the ability to determine a correlation is difficult.

UNDERSTANDING THE CONCEPT OF OUTLIERS

An outlier is an unexpected data point that is outside a normal or expected profile. Machine learning models have a difficult time incorporating these into a model. If we go back to the concept of regression analysis, it will help to understand the importance of outliers.

Logistic regression is the main concept used by neural networks. The accuracy of the correlation is based on creating a line or curve—in this case, that represents the data—and it is used to predict that a new data point will fall on or close to the delineated curve. Recall from chapter 5 that in figure 9, the line is based on the correlation that best fits the data.

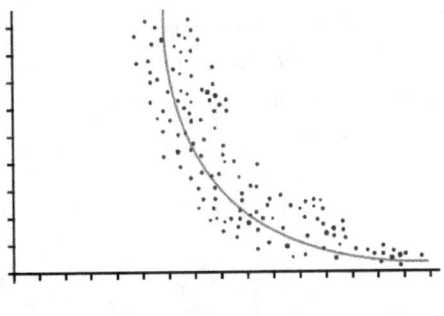

Figure 9

However, one or more points can cause a distortion in the curve. Should they be included in the curve or ignored? When they are unnecessarily included, it is called overfitting. A more accurate model can be created by ignoring these outliers, but at the same time, that reduces the accuracy of the model. This is why outliers in data are so important. Overfitting skews the model by trying to fit in outliers. Alternately the model ignores the outliers completely until they become significant enough that they need to be included.

In Figure 10 the line represents the closest correlation to the dataset by ignoring the two outliers. For this calculation, the algorithm ignores the new data points. As a result, the curved line does not truly represent all the data points.

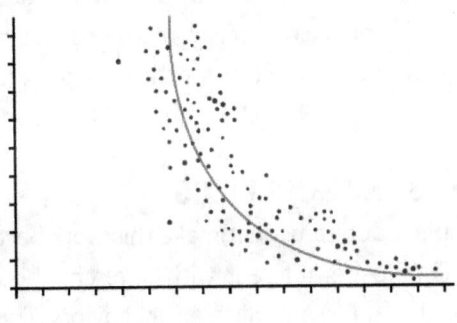

Figure 10

In Figure 11, the algorithm accepts one of the data points and read-justs the line to best fit the correlation of the data. When the algorithm includes outliers, it is called overfitting because it is trying to fit outliers into the model, which makes the overall correlation less accurate.

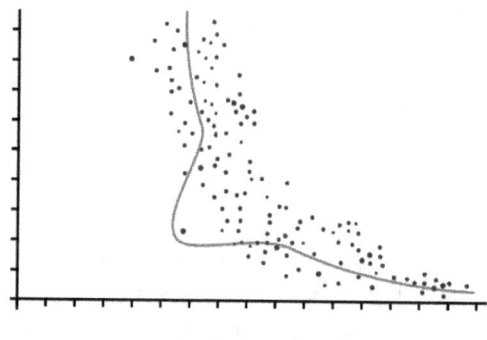

Figure 11

The point of all this is that it is important to create outliers in our personal data. This makes it difficult to be defined as part of a pattern. If the machine learning algorithm cannot detect a proper correlation, the reliability of the tool will be low, and the ability to predict the cor-rect response or action is also very low. Outliers create problems for machine learning algorithms that are trying to achieve a perfect cor-relation in the data. The algorithm tries to display a line that neatly represents the dataset. If you want to deceive AI tools by obscuring your personal profile data, then this is mathematically how you need to accomplish it. Your task is to disrupt the data patterns!

PROVIDE PERSONAL OUTLIERS

There is no simple list of items that make this work because every per-son is unique. People are different with different thought processes, different personality traits, and different behaviors. This means that a solution must be customized to you in a similar way that an AI tool creates a personality profile tailored to who you are. The way to deceive AI tools is based on your own unique characteristics and presenting data points that do not match. Instead of being on the extreme end of any trait, try to make sure you provide sufficient opposing data points that place you somewhere in the middle.

If it is not obvious, the first step is to make sure you understand a bit more about yourself and your personality. Go ahead and take a Myers-Briggs test and review your results. Or compare your personality to the Big Five personality test traits. Once you know what your expected profile should be, you can take countermeasures by providing opposite data points. If you are unsure, then ask a friend for feedback on your personality because it can sometimes be more difficult to recognize our own personality characteristics.

According to my profile analysis, I am an introvert. Fitting that profile, I normally do not speak or even contribute at large group meetings, preferring to provide my perspective in one-on-one situations. However, to provide an outlier, I check the meeting agenda beforehand, pick a topic, and study it. If one of the topics is about risk management, for example, I study information about one area of risk control. When the meeting happens, I pick my opportunity, and instead of saying nothing, I contribute a relevant comment, such as asking for further clarification or making sure there are risk owners for critical activities. It does not take a lot of work to quickly research any topic. For extroverts, confusing the data may mean remaining quiet, or looking at others in the room who don't often have the chance to speak and asking for their opinion.

Performing differently than expected can have consequences. If at one point during your workday, you send a burst of negative emails as an outlier, it can be detected and classified as a traumatic event that prompts further investigation. Other systems might flag the data points as unusual and create other issues. However, we must remember that when we deliberately provide outliers, the model becomes less accurate and is less reliable as a predictor of our behavior. We need to be aware that the model will lag any data trends until it decides to incorporate them as representative. A model can easily ignore one data point that does not match the model. A second data point can also be ignored. As more outliers are collected, the model must eventually take them into consideration and can create the new model that we seek to create.

Providing outliers can result in both good and bad outcomes; it depends on the type of outlier that is added to the system. I worked at an operations facility with numerous chemical and mechanical engineers. I was aware of one engineer whose manager was on the verge of firing him for poor performance. Two weeks before his annual performance review, the engineer discovered a cost savings that saved the company hundreds of thousands of dollars. This was a positive outlier, and he was retained. It also illustrates perfect timing, even though it was rumored that he acquired the idea from a coworker. If you provide outliers, the model has two choices: ignore the outlier or incorporate it. Both of these solutions create reliability problems when creating a person profile model.

SUMMARY

It is important to learn more about yourself and create data points that are not a true representation of your profile. This does not require numerous unique data points, as we see how a single outlier can confuse the algorithm. Both including and ignoring the outlier reduces the reliability of the results. More outliers make it more difficult to achieve a valid correlation, but we must be careful to avoid suspicion of a deliberate attempt to confuse the analysis software. In the next chapter, we not only provide outliers, but provide data points leading the algorithm to conclusions that we dictate. It supports our ultimate strategy to remove control from AI tools and give us the power to manage our own profile.

CHAPTER 9

Deception Strategy: Supply Personally Desired Data Points

In a work environment that uses AI as part of employee surveillance, it will be important for employees to find ways to manage their own profiles. This can be performed by training the AI algorithm with all your good habits and none of the bad ones. AI tools learn from data, so your task is to provide the best parts of you. If you feel any ethical concerns because you are being manipulative, then consider how invasive AI is and how the results can lead to unjustified negative consequences to your employment.

In creating your own desired data points, you can manipulate the model to include the outliers that you provide. The goal is to create data points that are given greater significance in the algorithm. Eventually the model will be reoriented toward the profile that you want the algorithm to achieve. Persistence is required because changing an existing model is not instant. The algorithm ignores outliers until they become too common to be excluded. At that point, the model makes the adjustment and considers them part of the correlation.

BUILDING THE PROFILE YOU WANT

You can build a false or "enhanced" profile by leading the data trend in a certain direction. To create a great profile, you supply the data that represents how you want to appear as an employee. This data shows your potential for higher positions. There are advantages and disadvantages to enhancing your profile or providing misleading data. If you are trying to enhance your personal profile, then your data points need to be classified correctly into the cluster that represents the image that you want to be. In order to deceive AI tools, you need to find a way to provide data that will result in the correlations that you want, and not random or even accurate data about your effectiveness as an employee.

In many work environments, a person's personality is given a much higher weight to their value to the organization than their performance. An employer might place a high value on employees who are confident, clever, and creative. They also tend to appreciate employees who can work as part of a team. If this is similar to your organization, then these are the data points that you need to provide. Your facial expression and words need to reflect these characteristics. Your body language, posture, and response to others all add up to data points that will create a better personal model. Smile when you meet people, and always smile or be serious in group settings. Your emails and text messages need to also reflect these qualities. Be positive and confident, even if you know something will fail. The language is important because AI tools don't always understand the context of common workplace situations.

Table 6: Neutral and Positive Communication Responses

Event	Neutral Response	Positive Response
Meeting or sending an email to senior managers	Listen passively and take notes. Answer evasively if asked a question.	• Smile and nod in agreement. • Praise latest initiatives. • Clearly state personal commitment to the organization.
Meeting or sending an email to team members	Provide updates.	• Praise latest initiatives. • Compliment a coworker. • Add adjectives such as *exciting*. • Recite accomplishments to date.
Meeting coworkers	Discuss non-work-related topics.	• Promote organization initiatives.

When I attended a company meeting held by the CEO, he explained to his entire staff that this private company had received offers to go public and that he proudly had turned them down. The CEO himself would have benefited the most financially by making the company public. I turned my head, covered my face, and rolled my eyes because I recognized some of his untruthfulness. I expected the company to become public, which it did in a short time after that talk. At a meeting with a different company, the CEO explained how well the company was doing, in spite of a huge debt load and dwindling sales. It was difficult for me not to shake my head in disbelief. The company declared bankruptcy within the next few months. For a strong profile, you need to smile and nod, even if you believe the truth is being distorted. In both of these situations, if I had been recorded by facial analysis, it would have provided negative data points in my personal model. For a strong profile, you need to smile and nod, even if you do not believe in the strategy or the message created by executives in an organization.

In terms of behavior data points, it is important to complete tasks on time or find reasonable means to defer or delay, as long as they are not considered your fault. Don't accept work tasks from others unless you are certain they can be completed on time and you will receive credit. Work in teams, but avoid dysfunctional teams. When working in teams, be sure that you have some personally assigned tasks that you can complete and for which you can receive credit. These are all positive data points that add to a profile. If you are worried about completing an assignment on time, find a way to add a risk that has not been previously identified. A risk means that the original task may not be achievable with the resources identified. Don't indicate to others that the task will fail, until it actually does. By sending a series of messages that your task is at risk of failure, you are adding a series of data points that will be taken negatively by the AI model.

When communicating, instead of using neutral words, try using more of the jargon of your organization. Also, find out the most popular, fashionable words, and sprinkle them in your communication. For example, you can write an email about an activity and then add how it is important to please the customer with the result. For general conversation, use the terms *artificial intelligence* and *statistics* more frequently. This will increase other people's perception of your abilities.

When using the internet at your workplace, you can click on links to relevant business books or ways to be more innovative, depending on the profile you desire. These are additional data points that might be useful. To enhance your profile, start following groups that align with your organization or business goals. For example, follow a company that works to improve team building, or join a leadership group to show that you have ambition and are willing to learn new skills. Find favorable professionals to connect to and like articles, with or without actually reading them. Browse for items that make you appear more professional, such as a new laptop or a store that sells business attire. Don't think about who are. Instead, think about who the organization wants you to be, and build that profile. Your image can be the young, ambitious, and energetic career professional, while your real self just wants to get through work every day and get paid.

Building that ideal profile requires that you also avoid certain sites. Review and reassess your browsing history weekly, and try to be consistent. For most organizations, it is expected and mandated that employees are not browsing certain websites during work hours. With AI tools, it goes a step beyond that. Everyone needs to avoid any site that would indicate that you are unprofessional on both personal and work networks. Pornography, juicy Hollywood gossip, and unusual beliefs (such as the world is flat) are inappropriate. Remember that most data collected is based on clicks and not on whether you actually read or follow anything. If you are a woman shopping for maternity items for your friend's baby shower, the tracker will think you are the one who is pregnant. Consequently, an unenlightened manager might start reducing the amount of interesting work projects assigned to you in preparation for you to take time off. Each day try to select something that shows you in the best professional image. You don't need to read the articles or books, and you don't need to buy anything. The tracker simply wants to see your preferences.

For external data points, build a good social media profile on LinkedIn, and hide your other profiles. If you have a Facebook profile that you use for personal connections, make sure it cannot be traced to you. Your Facebook photo should be disguised to the point that it cannot unlock your phone using facial recognition capability but that people can still recognize you. Similar to the suggestion in the section on providing outliers, you can create an avatar for social media and use that to hide any activities that you do not want to be traced. Your name on social media can be an abbreviation of your name. Use your middle name as your last name, or shorten your first name to an initial with your middle name. It makes it more difficult for data brokers to find you and creates confusion when trying to match the data to the correct person.

Remember when you performed a search for a specific item such as a pair of boots and then went to a store and bought them? For the next several weeks, all the internet ads you see are about boots because the tracking system did not get the message that you bought them. You search for a new camera, purchase it online, and still for the next several weeks you get ads for cameras. Maybe the tracker thinks you need two? The point of this is that you can lead a tracker to build the profile you want by deliberately clicking on things that you don't want. AI tools are becoming more sophisticated, so it is better to act now and stay one step ahead.

When I was a manager, checking applicants' résumés during the hiring process was very revealing. One person listed hobbies as cycling, swimming, and photography. Another person listed their favorite activities as playing team sports, singing in a choir, and helping organize charity events. From this, I could deduce that one enjoyed more introverted activities, and that the other was always involved in group activities. Of course, more information would be helpful, but if I interpret this the same way as a machine learning model, the data points indicate that one of them would be a better fit for tasks that require a single, concentrated focus and the other would be better working as part of a team. A computer can easily analyze these data points and make a judgment. Therefore, to confuse the analysis, each person should include both individual and group activity types in their personal data, which neutralizes the previous judgment.

How do we know which factors are given greater weight in the model? This is not easy, but one way is to feed a constant stream of data that has the same impact. If you want the model to view you as an extrovert, then provide those data points. The same philosophy applies if you want to shift the model or if you think the data points have created an image of your personality that you want to change. Start by providing a more constant stream of data that is reflective of what you desire. If you are sensitive and a little insecure but work in a tough business environment, then feed the model different data in order to be perceived as someone who fits well and will receive more opportunities and recognition in the organization.

A normal machine learning model must identify and eliminate historical bias in the creation of the model. *Historical bias* is the term used to explain that historical data can be flawed. For example, a model based on historical data might suggest that most people work in manufacturing and may not understand current trends in the workforce that indicate anything contrary, such as an increase in work in service industries. To deceive AI tools, we want to use bias as much as possible to help influence the results of the model. We can use bias by evaluating how closely we match the desired organizational employee. The closer we are, the less we need to feed the model fake data. We can also identify where we differ and feed fake data for that specific area of ourselves. Let's say the model has been capturing your personality for some time, including traits that you may not value or that you are working to improve. For example, if you want to be given opportunities to deliver presentations, you might take a course and then practice the skills in the real world. However, you need to feed the model some data points, or it will lag your progress and not offer opportunities at work for you to make presentations. The AI model is biased against you because you have no history of delivering presentations. Before AI tools existed, if you wanted to be seen as an excellent presenter, you would simply take a course and request the opportunity to practice. However, this is no longer the case.

SUMMARY

Instead of limiting the amount of data, a better option might be to feed false or slightly enhanced data points to the data collection tools. Once you describe the image you want, a plan can be created to use organization jargon at the most critical times. Instead of using neutral words, use positive words, and add positive body language. It will be easy to detect the most important times for manipulating these data points, such as in meetings and when interacting with senior staff. It is still essential to avoid specific behaviors both inside and outside the workplace. Supplying data points to create the personal profile that you actually desire is likely an easier and more positive approach when trying to deceive AI-based tools. A combination of limiting data points while providing your own desired data points is a sound strategy.

CHAPTER 10

Interpreting AI Results

A I programs use math equations to determine a result, and sometimes these results are very complex and require interpretation. Understanding and using the output of an AI program requires a good knowledge of statistics and will be beyond comprehension for most managers who use the AI-based tools. The math may also be beyond an average employee's knowledge. With that in mind, a review of the basics behind the math in AI-based programs is given in this chapter. If an employee can understand some of this knowledge, they will have an advantage and a better ability to deceive the algorithms. The software programs use equations based on different statistical methods and are used to evaluate the accuracy of the correlations in the data. AI software programs provide results based on probability and therefore are not always accurate. With any machine learning program, such as a neural network, an amount of interpretation of the outcome is required. Since interpretation is often subjective, this provides another opportunity to question the results of an AI program. If an employee provides inconsistent data points more frequently, it helps the plan to confuse AI tools and the results that are produced.

CORRELATION USING REGRESSION ANALYSIS

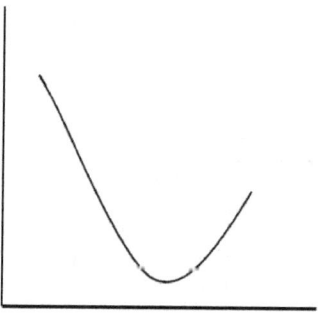

Figure 12

Calculating a correlation in a number of labeled datasets can be a complicated process. Yet, based on the result, an employer may take some action. A common algorithm is a neural network, which uses logistic regression to identify correlations in the data. Here is a simple example of how logistic regression works. The best correlation between a value, x, and a value, y, is at the lowest point on the curve in Figure 12. To find the lowest point, the software program starts with a value near the left side and top of the curve. It takes a second point on the curve and calculates whether the line has gone down or up, which is determined by whether the difference is a negative or positive value. It continues to go down the line until it reaches the lowest point, which is considered the best correlation. However, a neural network has to correlate all the data points, not just a single one, so it uses multiple logistic regression for the same dataset. This is the process of a machine learning program. It performs multiple regression on the data, and the best correlations are used to create a model, or a representation of the data. In finding the best overall correlation, there will be parts of the data that do not correlate as well. Part of deceiving AI tools is to create more of the poorly fitting data.

It can be difficult to determine exactly how a neural network makes correlations because the weights and biases used inside the program are continuously adjusted as part of the algorithm's process. Imagine a million pieces of data about you captured every day for a month. It will be difficult to understand what data points are more significant than others in creating your personal profile.

INTERPRETATION ISSUES

An AI program that uses a neural network to correlate data produces a probability value. For a personal profile, it might be the probability that your profile matches or is representative of a specific reference model. In statistics there is also a reliability factor that is similar to quoting political polling results. A machine learning algorithm can provide a probability of a 90 percent match, and in statistics we might say, for example, that the calculation is accurate nine times out of ten.

It is important to distinguish between a binary classification, which uses only two digits, a one and a zero, and a probability percentage. Using binary values can result in misleading outcomes. For example, if the probability prediction results in a value of 52 percent, then that value might be shown as a 1, or positive, because the value is greater than 50 percent. In a binary system, this indicates that any value between 50 percent and 100 percent has the same meaning, which is very unlikely. The problem is that decisions tend to be binary. We either take an action or we don't. Taking an action is a 1, and doing nothing is a 0. If we have a range of possible probability values, at what point is an action taken? Do we take action if the probability is 65 percent? A binary value means there nothing in between two choices. Do we have a headache or not? That is binary. The level of intensity of a headache can be a range of values. The purpose of these examples is to be aware that some conditions are binary, and some are better defined by a range of values. Employers and machine learning programmers find it easier to deal with binary data, but that does not always truly represent the results. As employees, it is good to be aware that actions or decisions can be taken by an employer based on inconclusive evidence.

Another mathematical issue is the accuracy of the probability results that are calculated using unbalanced datasets. This means in supervised learning, for example, that most of the datasets being fed to the model have the same label. If 99 percent of the datasets are labeled with a 1 result, then it is difficult for the model to assume anything different. I think of this as being stereotyped, with no way to change the outcome for as long as you work for the same employer. There are statistical methods to evaluate the detrimental impact of unbalanced labels in a dataset, but the problem remains that unbalanced data makes AI tools far less effective, and more work is required to validate if the outcomes are usable. It is another way we can provide data to disrupt data correlations.

One of the problems with correlating data is that the data provided might not be the actual reason for a correlation. In other words, it could be random, or in technical terms, it is not a *causal* correlation. For example, you evaluate all the successful construction projects in a country compared to those that were late or had huge cost overruns. There are many factors that can be considered, and let's say you included the company logo. The result showed that construction projects when the company logo was blue were far more successful. You have a correlation, but the color of a logo has no impact on the result. It is a random correlation. We can use this concept in how we provide our personal data by trying to add random data to the machine learning tools to confuse them. When building personal profiles, the data collected or the lack of data can result in a model that is not representative of an employee's personality. This can lead to problems when the response or direction given to an employee is based on random data and not a deliberate employee action or behavior.

SUMMARY

Interpreting the results of an AI program might seem simple, but that is far from the truth. The programs use equations that require an understanding of statistics, and different methods are available to evaluate the accuracy of the correlations. For prediction or classification, a probability value is provided. This is a critical characteristic that opens a way to question the accuracy of AI-based software programs. There will be a range of probabilities, and the lower the probability value, the less reliable the result. On the other hand, if the goal is to direct the programs to a desired profile, then the goal is to increase the probability of the result we want. As we develop a strategy to deceive AI tools, it is important to understand how correlation works and the importance of each data point collected. The software code that drives various AI-based programs may be inherently accurate, but the largest single impact on the result is the data.

CHAPTER 11

Managing an Employer's Objectives

This chapter looks at the organization's objectives and introduces some key strategies on how to derail machine learning results. It is helpful to narrow down the specific actions that you can take to achieve your personal objectives while also understanding what the organization strives to do. The typical objectives of the employer are in table 7.

Table 7: Typical Employer Objectives

Employer's Objectives
Improve productivity
Make good decisions
Maintain good morale
Deliver effective employee communication
Maintain good organizational image

EFFECTIVE STRATEGIES

The employer's main objective is to monitor and increase productivity. If you are not a top performer, then limit the amount of data that can be gathered, and supply data that shows good performance. If work is being done on several tasks in common, make sure that any task assigned directly to you is completed first. It is more difficult to find out where the problem lies when there are several people required to complete a task. If you want to manipulate AI tools and improve your profile, leave yourself logged into software programs or apps even while away from your desk. During lunch break, come back every ten minutes to click on a data field. Start watching a training or communication video, then leave it running while you take a break. It might be perceived that you are eating lunch at your desk, being very productive. Try not to leave the building if your location is being monitored or tracked with a security card for entry and exit. If you are being tracked, find out what device is being used; then give the device to a coworker while you are out for a long lunch and they stay at work. Alternately, leave the tracking device somewhere safe at your place of work.

I once worked for a large software company as a project manager in the professional services group. The organization had several very large business clients, and the executives routinely communicated with their counterpart executives in the client companies. This led to a lot of pressure because the executives rarely knew the project status or any problems. Their solution was to purchase workplace smartphones for employees. The smartphones tracked our movement and, of course, meant that we were always available, including weekends. On several weekends, my phone was forgotten in the top drawer of my office desk at work and, unfortunately, I may have missed a few calls. While I enjoyed the well-paid work, there were also times when I needed quiet time at home and to turn off the ever-present pressure of work activities.

As technology advances, new products will be developed that can be used to protect employee privacy. For example, a new ultrasonic bracelet has been designed to interfere with microphones picking up verbal communication.[28] While products that jam sound waves are not new, this device will jam any potential microphone or smart speaker activated in a workplace aimed to monitor employees. This is similar to blasting a loud song that blocks out all the words you are whispering to the person next to you, and it can be valuable as you move from one area to another. To avoid being obvious, you may need to encourage other coworkers to purchase the devices as well so that there is a critical mass of employees who use the device. It will be problematic if the employer bans the devices.

For employees who want to advance in the organization, completing tasks on time and showcasing your accomplishments is a good strategy to indicate how productive you are. However, if you find that you are being driven to overextend yourself by clever motivational techniques, you need to start providing outliers that will confuse the data profiling software. In order to avoid health issues, you can slow down your productivity or take sick days where you provide zero data points.

Also, for advancing in the organization, image will be important. Supplying all the proper data points showing that you are professional, supportive, and energetic is important. You can hide or minimize any negative characteristics and ensure your separate social media presence is not traceable to you. Find out what traits the organization values the most, and deliver those data points both through work activities and social media profiles.

---

28 Fingas, Jon. "Ultrasonic bracelet jams the microphones around you." Engadget. February 15, 2020.
https://www.engadget.com/2020-02-15-ultrasonic-microphone-jamming-bracelet.html

For the organization's objective of making good decisions, an employee can also rely on data. Making decisions based on data is a sound strategy, and that is essentially what machine learning algorithms are designed for. However, in some instances, the data might be corrupt, or the decision needs to be different based on other factors that the data did not include. In that situation, you make your own decision—the correct one—or blindly follow the data. At least when you follow the data, you will adhere to the AI model's expectation of your performance, even though it is a bad decision.

For organization morale, you can determine how you feel about and how you want to represent your employment in the organization. You can hide your true feelings with words and physical expression, but evaluating company morale normally depends on a larger sample of employees. If you believe the employer will present a new initiative if morale is low, you can encourage this by providing appropriately negative data points. However, some situations of low morale can be traced to a small number of individuals, and they can be targeted for negative consequences such as layoff or termination.

Communication in an organization tends to focus on one direction. Did the employee understand the communication? Organizations have tremendous problems communicating because they often use a generic message for all employees, which undoubtedly leaves some of them confused. There is a common expression, "You can't please everyone." With communication, the same saying applies. If you send the same message to every employee, it will not be universally understood and might be interpreted differently. The promise of AI-based tools is that customized messages can be sent to each employee. Therefore, if you want to deceive AI tools, reply that you do not understand your customized message. This confuses the AI tools. The assumption has to be that your personal profile is not correct or not reliable enough to create a message that can be easily understood. When a manager sends a message and the employee purposefully asks for clarification, the originator becomes uncertain about the content. This is a way that employees can manipulate and misdirect AI tools that are working to manipulate employees.

If you are not comfortable sharing how you feel about the organization you work for, use neutral terms whenever there is a discussion about the organization. This is one deception strategy that can easily be accomplished. In this situation, a lack of data is equivalent to a positive result. This is especially important if you are considering leaving the organization and being hired by a competitor. Leave your tracking device at work when going for an interview. If you are attending a remote interview, use a friend's home computer.

FEEDBACK IS YOUR DATA COLLECTION POINT

An important control point to verify how well you are achieving your objectives is feedback. In most organizations, feedback consists of two main activities. The first is the employee performance review, and the second is personal communication. Both of these are critical data collection points for you to assess what data has been collected and what type of personal profile is being used.

A formal performance review is often the most stressful event in a manager's workday. People are not born with an innate ability to fairly judge and effectively communicate with a person whom they rely on to complete tasks. It takes training, experience, empathy, and excellent communication skills to do this well, something that rarely occurs. In addition, preparation is crucial to being successful, and most managers are too pressed for time to prepare adequately. Now let's throw AI into all this. With AI, the manager might feel more confident because the results are customized for each employee, and there is likely a script to follow. Alternately, trying to deliver a message that is based on probabilities from a complex algorithm might increase stress and tension. Whatever the results are, it is important for an employee to view the performance review as an opportunity to gather information on what data is being collected, and whether you are being effective in managing your profile. Whether or not you receive a poorly conducted or well-conducted performance review, the written and verbal language of the review holds clues.

In a situation where you receive vague comments or inconsistent feedback, you are probably being successful at providing insufficient information or providing outliers that reduce the ability to use the profile successfully. The feedback you receive from an employer now provides double value. You can understand how your performance is being assessed and also how well you are deceiving the AI model of your personality profile. You can also use this as an opportunity to turn things around, by asking the employer questions such as, "What data did you base that on?" or "Is there data in your assessment of my performance that suggests that conclusion? I would like to find out more." These are tough questions because it is difficult to determine the exact data points and weighting used to determine a correlation. If you seek to be, or are working toward being, placed in a higher level within the organization, ask the manager whether they agree with your career objectives during the performance review. This should confirm that your profile is being modified successfully.

Many organizations attempt to provide ongoing feedback as a way to lower the stress of the formal review. This can be weekly or monthly, as a manager or team leader provides feedback. The way they choose to deliver the content should provide clues as to how effective you are at managing your profile. If you are trying to improve your profile, the results may be evident and possibly be a slight surprise to your manager, who may have a less-than-glorious outlook of you as an employee.

There are two organizational roles to consider. First, there is the creator of the AI algorithm that builds and modifies your personal profile. The creator is typically an information technology (IT) person who habitually creates machine learning algorithms for the organization.

It might be a person who is well versed in the creation and interpretation of results. If this person is involved, that is a positive factor. Interpretation can be very difficult with AI models, and a knowledgeable IT person can only indicate the level of accuracy or reliability of the model. These factors do not necessarily determine the effectiveness of the actions taken by management, which are based on the outcomes of the AI-based model. The algorithms produce probabilities and unfortunately, many IT people are not always mathematicians and do not have extensive background in regression analysis. In this case, the programmer might not understand the reliability issues or inaccuracies in the model.

The second character involved is the user of the results. This person is probably a direct manager who, with the assistance of a human resources representative, is trying to be more effective in employee communication and motivation. It can be expected that the manager has far less experience in understanding machine learning models and the regression probabilities than the creator of the software. It is most likely that they simply follow a formula based on the profile and some organizational procedure document that prescribes actions.

SUMMARY

An employer has several reasons to deploy AI technology in the workplace, and it may be beneficial for you to determine a strategy based on these organizational objectives. This is similar to the general ways of deceiving machine learning algorithms and making them less reliable. However, the difference is that the focus is on one or more of your specific personal objectives. Remember that employee feedback is your data collection point and is an opportunity to assess whether your strategy has made any impact on modifying AI-based analysis. If there are only subtle changes in your profile, it may be more difficult to determine whether you are successfully deceiving AI tools. Employee feedback can be vague and too generic, which probably means that the AI results are inconclusive or that they are too difficult to interpret properly. Regardless, the feedback received helps determine whether you have any level of influence or whether the AI tools control the direction of your work efforts.

CHAPTER 12

Who Owns Our Data?

The question that we need to ask ourselves is: "Do I own my personal data?" The answer is most likely, "No." Countries have various laws to protect people's privacy and also to protect creative content such as books and music. However, personal data is not classified as property and therefore has no owner. We know that data is important and that large organizations such as Facebook and Google collect it and find ways to monetize it. Although we do not own our personal data, it has value. Indeed, a stolen identity is worth something, or it would not be stolen and used.

Perhaps the most convincing proof that we don't own our personal data is the following example. A software business scoured the internet, using sites like Facebook and Instagram to collect over three billion photos of people with their names and reference fields, such as their locations. This data was used to create a massive database and was made available for purchase to more than six hundred law enforcement agencies. These agencies purchased access to the database and used it to identify people from a photo or video for their investigations. This was performed without the consent of or the notification to any of the individuals.[29] From countless examples such as this, we can assume that if we post our photo on the internet, it is free and available for others to use.

While we were researching the capture of personal data, one data broker advertisement stood out, claiming that they have collected over three thousand attributes for seven hundred million people. What kind of information are companies and data brokerages collecting on you? Everything they can. This ranges from the basic information that you might expect, such as your age and gender, to more personal and financial information, as shown in Figure 13. They probably know more about you than your doctor, your mother, and your best friend. If a company gives away anything to you that is "free," they are likely taking your personal information and selling it. Rather than us being compensated for it, companies are making millions of dollars from our data.

29   Kashmir Hill, "The Secretive Company That Might End Privacy as We Know It," The New York Times (The New York Times, February 10, 2020), https://www.nytimes.com/2020/01/18/technology/clearview-privacy-facial-recognition.html.

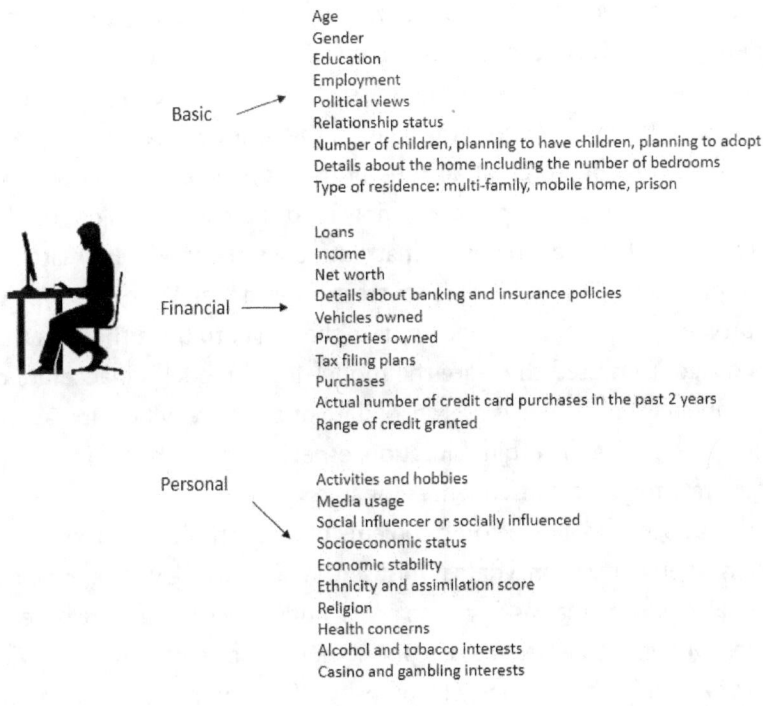

Basic
- Age
- Gender
- Education
- Employment
- Political views
- Relationship status
- Number of children, planning to have children, planning to adopt
- Details about the home including the number of bedrooms
- Type of residence: multi-family, mobile home, prison

Financial
- Loans
- Income
- Net worth
- Details about banking and insurance policies
- Vehicles owned
- Properties owned
- Tax filing plans
- Purchases
- Actual number of credit card purchases in the past 2 years
- Range of credit granted

Personal
- Activities and hobbies
- Media usage
- Social influencer or socially influenced
- Socioeconomic status
- Economic stability
- Ethnicity and assimilation score
- Religion
- Health concerns
- Alcohol and tobacco interests
- Casino and gambling interests

Figure 13

The data items listed in Figure 13 total around forty, and data brokers generally collect three thousand pieces of data per individual, so you can imagine other data fields that are not identified here.

Data security and privacy issues are ongoing concerns. However, these more popular issues mask the real problem, which is that our personal data has value, and it is taken from us without compensation. Sometimes the terms and conditions are so confusing and difficult to decipher that we just skip ahead to get a service, and then the business can go ahead and access our information. Organizations find ways to access our data or convince us to give it away for free. In most countries, we have a legal right to view our data—for example, our medical records or our personnel files stored by a human resources department. This becomes less practical when our data is held by an anonymous cloud-based computer storage device and we are denied access. What is even more troubling is that our data can be used and not captured or stored at all. One of the ways programmers use machine learning algorithms is to simply read the data to build a model, but not actually retain any of that data once the model is created. It simply needs to use the data to create the model. With this type of software program, we no longer have the ability to trace the data that the algorithm used to create the model. If the model is inaccurate or completely false, there is no trail of data or evidence of how it was created, which is a disturbing situation, especially if the model is used to generate negative consequences for an employee.

We see evidence of the problems of uncontrolled data proliferation when our personal data is misused. When we receive a telemarketer call or spam email asking us to reveal our financial assets, we have no idea who gained access to our phone number or email address. With new AI tools, these issues will intensify—for example, when our data is used to analyze our psychological profile and then to influence us in ways that we might not even be aware of.

If employees do not own their personal data gathered during their employment, they must be able to control it. But is it even possible to control data collection? Assuming that you have access to your data, the amount of time and technical knowledge required to manage the data is beyond the available time and existing skills of most employees. The largest issue that employees face now is how to control the data that an organization gathers. The ownership of personal data normally refers to both the possession and the responsibility to secure it. With machine learning tools, there is no longer any requirement for a business to possess the data, since as stated previously, the data can be read by an algorithm and not retained.

There is an increasing number of people who believe that personal data should be treated similar to property and protected, and that when data is used, the person should be compensated.[30] Legal protections are unable to keep pace with technological advancements that affect the intentional proliferation of personal data. For now, it falls to us to secure and protect it. We need to own and restrict the use of our personal data. At the very least, we need to secure it when we leave an organization. We need to be able to carry it with us, or at least receive a copy and have the original data erased.

ARE WE PROTECTED?

In the words of Davidow in the book *The Autonomous Revolution*, if I put a product on a shelf and someone takes it, it is called stealing and they might go to jail. If I put my data on the internet and someone takes it, then they are free to sell it to others without any consequences. Privacy of our personal data should be a fundamental right, and data protection is an important part of keeping it private. However, in an era of massive data collection, it seems impossible to stop our public and private data from being fed into AI-powered programs. Our inherent right to privacy doesn't matter in the digital world. The United Nations recently passed a rights declaration: *The right to privacy in the digital age.* The UN reaffirms the right to privacy, that "no one shall be subjected to arbitrary or unlawful interference with his or her privacy,

---

30 Will.I.Am, "We Need to Own Our Data as a Human Right–and Be Compensated for It," The Economist (The Economist Newspaper, January 21, 2019), https://www.economist.com/open-future/2019/01/21/we-need-to-own-our-data-as-a-human-right-and-be-compensated-for-it.

family, home" with the "rapid pace of technological development... [which] may violate or abuse human rights."[31]

This sounds nice, but words in a document don't protect users from having their data taken. Privacy protections depend on the country you live in and the company that you are dealing with. The United States appears to be lagging behind others concerning the issue of digital privacy and currently does not have any regulations that protect rights to privacy in a digital context. Europe, on the other hand, has adopted a new policy protecting consumers. Under the General Data Protection Regulation, users have to know, understand, and consent to their data being taken before companies can do so.[32] Pages upon pages of fine print to confuse the consumer and forcing users to click "yes" in order to sign up are no longer adequate. Instead, if a company wants to obtain a client's personal data, they have to explain in clear language why it is needed, how long they will be using it, and how long they will be keeping it.

Table: 8 AI and Human Rights

Country/Body	Law/Act	What This Does	Level of Protection
United Nations	UN: Right to Privacy in the Digital Age	Reaffirms our right to privacy in the digital age.	This does not force companies or countries to follow this.

31   United Nations, "Right to Privacy in the Digital Age," OHCHR (United Nations General Assembly, December 18, 2013), https://www.ohchr.org/en/issues/digitalage/pages/digitalageindex.aspx.

32   European Union, "Principles of the GDPR," European Commission—An official website of the European Union, June 7, 2019, https://ec.europa.eu/info/law/law-topic/data-protection/reform/rules-business-and-organisations/principles-gdpr_en.

| Canada | Personal Information Protection and Electronic Documents Act | Protects consumers; requires companies to gain consent before taking data. | Applies to any commercial enterprise that collects personal data during business; however, the retention of cookies is up to the individual browser.[33] |
| Europe | General Data Protection Regulation | The consumer has to consent to their data being taken before a company can. | More effective; the power balance is shifted toward consumers. Companies have to explain why they are collecting information and for how long. |

Whether a government wants to increase its surveillance, or a company wants to target a certain demographic for its ads, it is all about the data. Countries such as China are presumed to be getting more data on its citizens because of the type of government. Governments as well as businesses are already implementing facial recognition technology to monitor their citizen's social credit scores and identify and locate certain individuals.

The use of AI disproportionately impacts marginalized populations, which can include women, children, certain racial groups, ethnic groups, and members of the LGBTQ+ community.[34] The increased

33   Bennett, Chris, Tyson Gratton, and Jason Yao. "Website Cookies in Canada: Is Consent Required?" Lexology, April 2, 2020. https://www.lexology.com/library/detail.aspx?g=9a2dd4b7-bf75-4957-ac97-331ac98cebca.

34   Access Now, "Human Rights in the Age of Artificial Intelligence," AccessNow.org (Access Now, 2018), https://www.accessnow.org/cms/assets/uploads/2018/11/AI-and-Human-Rights.pdf.

use of AI in the criminal justice system leads to more defendants of a specific race labeled as high risk, given tougher bail conditions, and convicted with longer sentences. AI software is used in the United States to score detainees at every stage of detention, and one of the results is that governments are handing over their decision-making to private software vendors.

Data is one of the world's most valuable resources, and collecting data is also a high priority for businesses. If you agree to work for a company that has employed AI for measuring employee response and production rates, and later were to dispute the amount of data they are collecting, you will probably not have any justifiable grounds. There are very real implications to not following workplace norms. It is unlikely that you can get relief by having a reasonable conversation with your manager, trying to explain that you don't want the company to be monitoring your performance with AI and that you should be protected by privacy laws.

OUR RIGHT TO DATA PRIVACY

AI tools need data to function properly, and that means they need to constantly find ways to gather and use everyone's personal data. If is it not given willingly, there are ways to influence people to provide it. People might be naive or simply innocent in believing that our trust will not be abused. An app asks, "Can we use your location?" or a website posts, "We use cookies," and we simply click "I Accept" and move along to what we are trying to do. If you want access to a website for a "free" report, you need to register. Part of that is normally a request for your phone number and email address. Location data is probably the easiest data to collect because it is automatically included in a smartphone. We simply have to agree to share it using any app, and it becomes available. Location data calculates where you are, the duration of your stay, and all of the routes for your travels.

In many cases, we are asked for our data in return for a reward. This is the most dangerous kind. We sign up for a points card, and suddenly an AI tool is used to analyze every purchase at every moment in time. On the bright side, I received an email that one of my fresh vegetable purchases was recalled due to E. coli contamination and should not be eaten. It took me a while to realize that they knew from my grocery store points card exactly what I purchased, when I made the purchase, and where I made the purchase. Credit cards also collect points on our behalf, which mean that they collect an enormous amount of data. They show any purchases, returns, the date, and the location, or as certain marketers like to call it, a shopping pattern. Of course, we agree to the terms and conditions, but how many of us read through the terms and conditions carefully and then ask to remove a section that we are not happy about? The reality is that if you need to sign up for a credit card, you will automatically lose control of your purchasing data.

The most successful way to acquire personal data from us is the promise of convenience. Instead of entering a series of numbers, facial recognition can easily unlock your phone. A virtual assistant can read an incoming message requesting a meeting, add it to your calendar, alert you when it is time to leave, and select the most convenient route to the destination based on weather and traffic conditions. When you call a business or connect by chat, the first point of contact for customer service is normally an AI-powered agent. They interpret the context of your verbal or written expression, and either answer themselves or pass it to a live person for more difficult issues. The point is that they analyze every communication that you provide. While this may be helpful to resolve your customer service problem, it also means that they capture and dissect your communication. Once again this includes interpreting sentiment and emotions based on the communication, words, and context.

There was a trend a number of years ago in which people collected their personal information and stored it in a virtual safe.[35] This is not the best way to protect it, as it is likely only a partial copy of the data with the rest spread across the internet or in an organization's database. By creating a virtual safe, people are identifying only critical pieces of their data and declaring that to be the basis of their identity. In other words, they claim that the only *true* profile that can be created must be partly based on the data that they certify.

Claiming the rights to our real data might be a way to fight back. If we all were to identify critical pieces of information and validate our profile data, this may allow us to legally challenge a profile that causes negative consequences for us, especially if it is not based on personally certified data. Additionally, if an employer's profile is based only on a small amount of corrupt data, there is more of an argument to dismiss the negative consequences. Of course, there is a lot of uncertainty around how this would work, and the concept is far from being fully developed. At this stage, we need to find ways to protect ourselves. If we can validate our profile and claim our data, this might be the start of a strategy to make it happen. It will take a large community of individuals, as well as legal support. Currently, there is no way to control our profiles, and profiling based on our data remains a wild, open landscape with very few, if any, restrictions.

Numerous countries have a freedom of information act or access to information act that allows legitimate requests to receive a response for information, typically created by a government organization.[36] In this situation, whenever a person outside the government organization

---

35 Lucas Mearian, "Bank Offers Virtual Safe-Deposit Boxes for Storing Data," Computerworld (Computerworld, February 19, 2001), https://www.computerworld.com/article/2590794/bank-offers-virtual-safe-deposit-boxes-for-storing-data.html.

36 Dyfed Loesche, "Infographic: More Countries Adopt Freedom of Information Laws," Statista Infographics, November 9, 2017, https://www.statista.com/chart/11757/more-countries-adopt-freedom-of-information-laws/.

makes a request, a government agency needs to respond. If you happen to work for a government or related organization, this has repercussions on your data being shared. During an access to information request, an agency can request access to search your emails, including those that have been archived. The response may necessitate investigation of both workplace emails as well as any personal emails that can be accessed if they were created and sent on an organization's computer system.

As an employee, there are privacy controls in which an organization must protect an employee's data but also must reveal what personal data is being collected, why it is being collected, and the purpose or results obtained from using the data. Employees may feel awkward asking to see this type of information, as it might be viewed as an aggressive tactic by an unhappy employee or someone who does not share the organization's goals and values.

SUMMARY

We need to own the rights to our data and understand the value that it now holds. With no legal protection, the best we can do is to contaminate our data. We like to think that our data is protected or that we are careful with disclosing our personal data, but the reality is there are those who help themselves without our consent and acquire our data for financial gain. It is legal to collect, track, and even sell data. We don't own our personal data, and the only restriction for data collected during employment is internal company polices, if they even exist. Don't forget that organizations also share our personal data with others under agreements that are supposed to protect us, but they are really only providing protection for the organization.

Persuading someone to give access to their data has reached a high level of sophistication that is often impossible to refuse. There needs to be significantly more resistance before anything changes, which is unlikely, given that our ability to avoid succumbing to the influence of rewards and convenience is low. Our personal data has value, and we need to all internalize that lesson.

CHAPTER 13

A Typical Workday Managing Your Data

Assume that you receive work messages that are far too psychologically persuasive, and you want to be able to resist the suggestions more easily. The best response to manage this situation is to reduce the number of data points and provide more outliers. Regardless of whether you work in a physical workplace or work remotely, you need to modify your daily routine. How you spend your day will be different for different locations, type of employment, and job requirements, but data from your daily activities will be captured in all these environments.

As mentioned in the technical section, the most common machine learning method is supervised learning, which means that the datasets are labeled. When creating a personal profile and using supervised learning, the data collected is first classified into a personality type or psychological profile before it is used. One way to disrupt the model is to provide data labeled as a data point that is extremely different from your personality. The plan is to create outliers that the algorithm has difficulty classifying. This reduces the probability that the calculated correlations are accurate, which makes the model less reliable and less useful. We can also use outliers to our advantage to skew the data so that the model represents the profile that we want to be seen and used.

PROVIDING ERRATIC DATA POINTS

There are many ways to provide outliers. If you have a consistent arrival time each day at work, and the first thing you normally do is sit for thirty minutes answering emails, you need to provide a different pattern. To provide outliers, open up a different application, such as a spreadsheet, or take a break to walk around and talk to colleagues. Instead of reading all your email at the start of the workday, search the titles, and randomly choose a few to read and reply. Make sure any replies are brief, and use neutral words.

In a scheduled meeting with coworkers, you may choose not to speak at all. If asked a direct question, keep the answer short and neutral. You can always suggest that you will follow up later with an email, which allows you time to express the intent you want. If you want to improve your profile, do not use any negative facial expressions. You can smile or act excited if a new change is announced, regardless of what it is. If the meeting uses a video platform such as Skype or Zoom, you need to be careful regarding your facial expressions. If you want to completely confuse the sentiment analysis tool, you can smile and scowl over the same topic. If you are not physically in a room with people during the meeting, you can block your camera and only show your photo or avatar on the screen.

Writing an email is the best opportunity to create input for a sentiment analysis tool. Remember that you want to put in outliers to confuse the model so that there is a lower possibility of being manipulated by the AI tools. Instead of suggesting a change to a task description, for example, you can write that the task is interesting and may need to be reviewed. You can also use words that sentiment analysis tools will misinterpret. To confuse AI tools, avoid saying that a task is not going well. Instead, try a story such as "I saw a dog outside yesterday, and it pooped on my lawn. This task is like that." For emails that need a reply, check your personal dictionary of positive, neutral, and negative words and phrases that you can use to create a response. Use neutral words if you are engaged in chat sessions with other employees, and avoid any non-work-related items.

It is always good to complete tasks you are assigned. If you are assigned a task to create a new document that normally takes two days, work on it offline, and when you upload your text, it will show as being completed in far less time. This creates an outlier. However, you do not want to have a lot of these data points because it will turn into an expectation. Go to LinkedIn and click on a couple of relevant business or technical articles without reading more than the title.

When you want to connect with friends or deal with personal issues, leave the building and use a personal smartphone. Avoid using the organization's Wi-Fi, which can capture your communication. It is ideal to connect with coworkers during breaks or lunches, which will also make the employer happy because you are not doing this during regular work time. Breaks and lunch are also good times to discuss non-work-related items with coworkers, but you still need to be careful to avoid descriptive adjectives and certain topics that can be captured and used to create a psychological profile.

Table 9: Examples of Managing a Profile

Creating a "good" employee profile	Creating a "bad" employee profile
• Log into workplace software constantly during the day	Fail to complete assigned tasks within a reasonable time

• Avoid personal social media activity using detectable devices	Post regularly on social media with friends and watch non-work-related cat videos
• Like and comment on the organization's social media content	Ignore organization's social media posts
• Outside of work hours: Share appropriate articles and like posts from relevant professionals	Outside of work hours: Connect with inappropriate groups and display questionable behavior

We all have common habits, and evidence of that is already being captured by our technology devices. For example, if you have an Apple Watch connected to your iPhone, the iPhone is collecting your data—mainly your daily habits. If you use your phone to frequently check the weather, your Apple Watch face will automatically change to include a weather display. If you are frequently checking the stock market, the Apple Watch will change the watch face to include the stock market. Personally, I find this annoying, but it illustrates how easy it is to monitor your habits and also how you have a common set of behaviors in your everyday life that you may not even be aware of. The goal is to deceive these data capturing mechanisms by recognizing your habits and breaking that pattern. This is a simple strategy for influencing the data you provide. It requires deliberate action, not simply continuing your day without realizing how you produce identical behavior patterns every day. It does not require you to be a different person, only to provide a number of new or different data points.

With a work-supplied smartphone, the employer knows when you are on your way to work and approximately what time you will arrive based on GPS location tracking. If you have a phone provided by the organization, you can leave it with someone you trust or leave it at your desk for part of the day. If you don't have a desk, then leave it in a jacket pocket with the jacket hung in a specific location, and move around without it. You can also leave it at home for a day or pretend you misplaced it.

When you use your employee badge to enter a building, the employer knows exactly when you arrive. If an employee badge is not used on entry, then a video camera might be used to capture everyone entering and will identify your face from the video and attach a time to the data. The software tracks the duration from your entry to the time you first access your computer at your desk. If you are working remotely, the employer's tracking software identifies your first connection to the work environment by any other means, such as a computer login or accessing email on your smartphone. When you review all unread emails as your first task in the morning, the system already knows what is in your inbox and begins to analyze which ones you respond to first. The software captures what you consider to be the priorities. It also analyzes your response and builds an assessment of your sentiment toward each sender.

This is no guarantee that any day's activities will produce a lower reliability model. It takes ongoing effort, and that can be a burden. It is important to check on any feedback provided and let that guide you as to how aggressive you need to be with your plan. Finding ways to completely block tracking of your activities at work is probably a bad idea. The missing data about you will be obvious, in comparison to the large amount of data collected from other employees. The lack of data will become suspicious, and the most likely response will be someone telling you to stop and will result in negative perceptions, which is not a great way to manage your deception. A better strategy is to use more drastic measures at specific times, such as when you do not want your employer to capture what you are doing. For example, you can turn off the employer's access to screen capture for a short time. While there is software that can do this, the reality is that this changes all the time with new vendors, as well as advances in software. The employer's software will need to allow access to screen sharing somewhere in your computer settings. This is what your personal software will turn off so you can have a moment of privacy. To fool network monitoring, you can also acquire encryption software so that everything from you passing across the network is unreadable. Once again, this is a severe solution that the employer will eventually discover, so care needs to be taken on how this is used. There is no single solution. The best way to work through the technical aspects is to search the internet for the most recent techniques to set this up.

Working remotely, either on a regular basis or part time, has similar if not the same issues. An employee still needs to complete tasks, send emails, and communicate with others. There are, of course, unwritten rules of email, such as never using all caps, which indicates that you are yelling. What's worse, reading or sending an email without ever having the recipient physically in front of you can result in unintended misinterpretation. When I receive an angry email, one strategy I use is waiting to reply and thinking about the reaction to my response before actually responding. The second method I use is to imagine that one of my good friends, Mike, is the sender. Mike was such a good guy that my anger always subsides, and I can respond in a more normal and straightforward tone. This is a good strategy to use when responding to work messages. Consider the content and understand how to respond based on your plan of limiting data, providing outliers, or supplying desired data points.

Another strategy that can be used when working from home or remotely is to be more available. At one point, my workplace became toxic, and I requested that I be allowed to work remotely full time. I set up a home office. I was located in Canada, and my manager was in the United States. My request was allowed, and I was determined to make it a successful transition. I was logged in to the organization's application at normal work times, and my phone rang with my work phone number. Several months into remote working, my manager made one of his regular phone calls, and I answered immediately. He sounded surprised and admitted, "Paul, I know you work remotely, but whenever I call your number, you answer, and whenever I send an email, you send a response almost immediately. I get better response from you than I do with my employees who are actually working in the office." There was no workplace surveillance at that time, but I provided enough positive data points to impress my manager.

DEALING WITH COWORKERS

According to a Gartner survey, the proportion of large corporations using employee monitoring in 2015 was 30 percent. This rose to 50 percent in 2019 and is expected to quickly rise to 80 percent. Organizations can justify this monitoring because of existing and ongoing employee deception. One survey reveals that 55 percent of employee manipulation is to make themselves look better. To accomplish this, they falsify data, inflate their performance numbers, and change timesheets. In addition, 31 percent of the incidents are examples of trying to make their colleagues look bad, such as taking credit for their ideas and withholding information about important meetings.[37] This helps to explain why organizations implement employee monitoring, which is to encourage more honesty.

Researchers also studied why employees engaged in this type of behavior. Employees were motivated to improve their performance to take advantage of opportunities for better work and promotions. They viewed it as a competitive environment with rewards for those who are perceived as having better performance. This is a lesson for our attempts to deceive AI. An employee can gain workplace competitive advantage by deliberately modifying the data collected and ultimately

---

37 Jagannathan, Meera. "These Are the Employees Most Likely to Cheat at Work." MarketWatch. November 17, 2017. https://www.marketwatch.com/story/these-are-the-employees-most-likely-to-cheat-at-work-2017-11-17-12881138.

the machine learning model profiles, especially if others are not following the same tactics.

One of the more obvious problems in managing deception is coworkers who may ask you questions about your odd or erratic behavior, especially when you are planting outliers. The good news is that your behavior should be consistent for a majority of the time. If a coworker is also considered a friend, then you may want to let them know what you are doing. They might think you are a victim of some strange conspiracy theory, or they might understand what you are doing. They may even join you or hopefully support you. It will be more troublesome if they are promoted, become your manager, and start to use the AI tools knowing what you are trying to accomplish with deceptive behavior. For other coworkers, it may not be noticeable if your main interaction with them is through email, text, or a workflow tool being used by a group of employees.

Once coworkers find out about employee profiling, they might start their own campaigns of deception. This is a positive development and will make your behavior seem less of an outlier. The profile being created about you is based on your personal data and is not affected by the behavior of others. The overall impact is likely to be the creation of less effective models for all employees. If management discovers the plot, they will consider what actions to take. They can reprimand employees for being deceitful in the workplace based on specific data points. Otherwise, as mentioned previously, it will be difficult for them to ask employees to act more like themselves. Understanding that certain data points are outliers, any actions taken by an employer to make manual adjustments in the profile are more likely to mess up the math than improve the accuracy of the profile. Building and using machine learning models is a complex process.

DECEIVING OUTSIDE THE WORKPLACE

Can these strategies to deceive AI tools also be used to manage AI tools used outside the workplace? Currently, AI-based software used for general market data collection, such as with credit cards and points cards, is far more sophisticated. However, these tools don't have the consistent daily data capture that occurs with work-performance data. Why bother trying to deceive AI outside a workplace? Deceiving AI tools outside of the workplace is fairly easy for most people. For example, when you purchase a book on Amazon, it is easy enough to ignore the recommendation list or update your preferences. Sometimes you might be tempted with an irresistible offer; however, it is usually easy to review the content and make your own judgment. I frequently receive emails or social media requests to register for an online course. It is easy to ignore the request, and at some point, the marketing program will make an adjustment based on the low success rate. The biggest challenge is when the messages become irresistible and I find myself making purchases that I later regret. It is similar to a convincing sales pitch being used by a person, in which you are cornered by a strategy that results in a positive response. A larger issue is that machine learning profiles reveal the types of people who are more psychologically vulnerable and easily convinced to make unwanted purchases. While the excuse is that everyone has free will, there is an ethical issue with predatory practices. In order to deceive AI tools, the same principles as those suggested in the workplace apply outside the workplace. The advantage outside the workplace is that you are relatively free to create the social profiles you prefer.

One way to confuse AI tools outside the workplace is to hide your social media profile. You can rearrange your name, use a nickname, and use an avatar for a photo. A disadvantage is that you might not be found on social media by acquaintances and may also confuse potential friends. Similar to the work environment, you can provide profile misdirection by clicking on items that you do not want to purchase and articles that you have no interest in. These become outliers that make your profile less accurate. Be careful about the data you provide anywhere on the internet because data brokers will access it. You can try listing two different personal data points in two different locations, in which you list one age in one location and a different age in another location, and the web scraper will have difficulty matching it to the same person. It can be very frustrating when you are not able to be yourself, but the benefit is that you won't be stereotyped. However, the messages you receive will be easier to reject because the profile created will not be effective at understanding your psychological traits or your purchasing preferences.

If you seriously want to limit the profiling, the first step is to limit the amount of online data you provide. This includes social media sites as well as business sites that ask for data. Perhaps it is your landlord, electricity payment, or your grocery shopping points card. Be deliberate about what you provide and what sites you are going to use for social media. Also remember that every click on the internet is traceable unless you use a private browsing function. Another advantage of limiting your online data is that you may actually find out who is selling your data. When I purchased a new sofa at a local furniture store, they asked for my address and phone number for delivery. Two days later, I started receiving scam phone calls after a long period of receiving none at all. Since I don't normally hand out my phone number and haven't in many years, I knew it came from this purchase. The furniture store either sold the data or had insufficient security for their database.

AI tools used outside the workplace are far more powerful and invasive, because retailers have a lot to gain from these tools. Revenue generation from email marketing and online recommendations are so high that there are continuous improvements being made to make the tools even more powerful. This is known as customized marketing, and it has the ability to make influential suggestions that generate an extremely high level of discretionary purchases. It is best to avoid these sites during your workday.

SUMMARY

The plan for your typical workday is to be slightly more inconsistent in your habits. Vary the patterns that you normally set. The concept is not to be someone else, but to create uncertainty in which category defines you. Coworkers help to create the culture of the organization, and sometimes this means embellishing their accomplishments. Data will always be collected, and you need to determine which coworkers can be trusted and which ones are planning their own personal agendas.

Inside a workplace, the use of AI-based software is for productivity, which makes the organization more financially efficient. Outside the workplace, AI tools are used to increase the amount of money that people spend on products. In both situations the objective is to make the tools more powerful and difficult to resist. The ability to deceive all AI tools is based on the same principles of reducing information, providing misdirection, and deliberately offering outliers. Your objective is to take control of your data and be able to make your own decisions in the world, not ones that are based on being severely influenced by a software program.

CHAPTER 14

Be Ethical

The deception so far has been rather harmless in terms of legal liability or even organizational tolerance. However, there are other more devious ways that may cross the line into unethical or illegal activity. This type of strategy cannot be condoned and is very difficult to accomplish. There is no justification for illegally attempting to cause damage to AI tools. This content describes the difficulty in attempting this and the complications that may result.

CHEATING

One way to defeat workplace surveillance using machine learning algorithms is to sabotage the results. Since some algorithms will be internally created, while others are software programs acquired from a vendor, this would require someone knowledgeable about the programs being used and how they are controlled. The most successful approach is to disrupt or corrupt the database that contains your information. There will be a database that collects information and then sorts it into various employees for input into the analysis tools. Altering the data in the database is the most direct approach to manipulating the profile and is easier than trying to change or corrupt an actual software program. Injecting new data or changing data in a variety of data fields is less likely to be noticed. Deleting data might be difficult and is more likely to be noticed by the organization.

Doing any of this, however, requires an understanding of data management. Machine learning software only reads data; it does not store or create any. The data is provided from a database that may or may not be updated regularly. However, any of these tactics to alter a database will contravene organizational policy and are probably illegal. With today's secure information technology infrastructure, it may even be impossible to find the raw data that feeds your personal model.

A better alternative, if you manage to find and replicate your raw data, is to create your own software program that is a parallel AI model. Of course, you need to understand the data and how it is being used, as well as how to program a machine learning algorithm. If successful, you can determine the set of data to provide that will achieve the results you want. This is accomplished by feeding different data to the algorithm and determining the greatest impact on the outcome. It is a lot of work and requires in-depth knowledge of how to use software to create a model that not only correlates your data but also compares it to other models.

FIND A BETTER WAY TO CONTROL AI TOOLS

If you are planning to implement some of these suggestions, you are likely to be discovered and face serious consequences. Stealing data and changing code to corrupt an algorithm are against business policy and will likely result in termination and possibly legal action. Instead of trying to corrupt an algorithm or a set of data, you can work toward becoming the person who can successfully manage the creation and use of these tools. If you have the skills to understand what you are trying to do with the AI tools, you will be in demand in many organizations. These skills are highly desired and difficult to acquire. Becoming knowledgeable about building machine learning based profiles might not be your most desired career path, but it offers an interesting opportunity and probably much higher pay.

If someone discovers that an employee is purposefully manipulating their profile, it will be difficult for anyone in the organization to mandate any consequences. How will anyone know that an employee is purposefully providing outliers, especially if they are new to the workplace or working remotely? It will be difficult to prove that they manipulated the results because doing so requires an understanding of these tools, an unusual skill for an average employee. The people responsible for data collection can only ask you to be more like your true self, which sounds absurd.

Many organizations have a policy that describes ethical behavior for employees. Deliberately leaving a smartphone with another employee so your location cannot be tracked might be considered a policy infraction. However, forgetting your smartphone at your desk because your colleague asked you to go for coffee sounds like something everyone may do at some point. There is a distinction between typical behavior and deliberately engaging in behavior to provide fake results. Reducing the amount of data about yourself by taking some of the actions mentioned previously, such as not using a work account for personal emails, is a sensible alternative and theoretically might be endorsed by an employer.

When an organization captures social media data about you, it is borderline in terms of ethics. There is, of course, some responsibility outside the workplace to be professional, and this might depend on your position in the organization. However, your personal likes or habits outside the workplace are not usually part of the organization's concern. Creating a fake profile and hiding activities from the organization, as long as they are legal, are beyond organizational policies. While there is a lot of freedom in protecting your data without concern for serious organizational repercussions, workplaces still do capture large amounts of data about the personal lives of employees. Organizations are known to collaborate with others in certain areas, and if you lose your job, you might discover that your tactics have been shared and no one in the industry will hire you.

The true fear from tampering with AI is if you are actively trying to access and alter an organization's databases and algorithms. Being vigilant with the amount of personal data you expose at the workplace or away from work is a better strategy. Reducing the amount of personal data and becoming a sterile presence in the organization is simply good sense for any employee.

SUMMARY

The methods suggested in this chapter are not meant to encourage anyone to take this approach because it is likely to result in some form of reprimand, termination, or possible prosecution. A better option is to challenge the organization and the results as being inaccurate. If you gain sufficient knowledge about AI-based tools, you will not need to take such a serious risk in creating and implementing a strategy of deception. It is not sufficient to justify any unethical action based on an organization's generous collection and use of personal data fed into a statistically imperfect algorithm. Think carefully before you select this path because there can be other consequences that are not evident.

CHAPTER 15

The Opportunity for AI Self-Destruction

Technology is never perfect, and AI is no exception, especially considering the complexity of the process for designing and implementing a workplace solution. There are numerous reasons why the technology will fail or simply become unusable. Some of these reasons for failure can be accelerated by our plan for deception, while at other times, the technology simply provides disappointing results, and the implementation is terminated. Rather than do nothing and hope for failure, a better choice is to follow a plan and believe that we had a small part in the downfall.

UNRELIABLE AI OUTCOMES

There are additional factors that can produce an unreliable model without your involvement. First, the vendor software or internally created algorithms must function appropriately. Machine learning models are more than programming and frequently need a mathematician to understand, interpret, and tweak the programming code. This is a new technology, and traditional IT groups are likely to have difficulty implementing this type of software.

Implementing AI requires a strategy as well as a process model. The process includes data collection, the machine learning code, processes to back up the data, processes on how to use the data, standards on what level of reliability is acceptable, and a process for constant data updates. Even with a well-defined strategy, there may not be sufficient data to create a model. Lack of data is typically one of the most significant reasons why AI implementation does not meet expectations.[38] Collecting data is more than scraping data from a variety of sources. As mentioned previously, data needs to be cleaned and in a standard format. Databases can be difficult to manage, and with the volume of data needed for AI, it will be an even greater challenge.

Sometimes the data cannot be correlated well enough to make an accurate prediction. If we feed the algorithm sufficient false or slightly inaccurate data, then our personal profile model will show a low percentage of reliability. Machine learning algorithms rarely achieve a 100 percent correlation, and this results in a probability value that the correlation is accurate. A neural network uses regression to correlate the data, and there are circumstances and interpretation errors that make the results questionable. The output from an AI-based program is typically a probability value, and someone needs to understand what ranges of values are acceptable when making a decision or taking an action. If a result is 95 percent, that is a lot more certain than a value of 74 percent. How do you make judgments based on the various ranges of values that are possible?

38 Quora, "Is Data More Important Than Algorithms," Forbes, Jan 26, 2017, https://www.forbes.com/sites/quora/2017/01/26/ is-data-more-important-than-algorithms-in-ai/#2d6d3d1542c1.

Even when the model gives a high probability value, it requires validation. For example, think of consumer or voter surveys in which they state that the results are accurate nine times out of ten. The same criteria apply to a machine learning model. On the other hand, using a result based on a low reliability model has the possibility of creating unforeseen or unintended consequences. If probabilities were always correct, sports teams would not need to play the games. Yet we know of many occasions where the underdog was victorious. With an improperly used AI algorithm, there will be no underdogs. Our future lives will be influenced in such a way that they are cast in a mold that becomes unbreakable, even though the model used was only based on statistical probabilities.

Proper use and interpretation of AI results requires a background in math and statistics. These are fields in which there is a scarcity of talent and experience. It is likely that AI-based solutions will fall to people who are told to follow a series of standard practices and procedures. They will be unaware of the issues of model reliability but are likely to proceed regardless. AI tools can be used by practitioners who are more concerned about results than accuracy. Employers might bypass any conditions that hinder the ability to use the algorithms, and as a result, employees will become the victims of these inaccuracies.

In order to compare personality profiles to a psychological model, the systems and interfaces need to be constantly updated and maintained. A process also needs to be defined on how all this will work and the responsibility given to a manager who will interpret and use the data. There needs to be verification of the results in the form of a feedback loop that determines whether the actions taken have been effective, and the level of effectiveness. In order to manage the outcomes properly, there also needs to be rules-based logic attached to the AI tools. Rules-based logic is similar to an expert system. The logic dictates that, if a certain event happens, the correct response or the response that will most likely result in the desired outcome will be applied. It is similar to the way a self-driving vehicle works. If the vehicle sees an image of a stop sign, the rule says it must stop. If the self-driving vehicle determines there are no obstacles, the AI makes a decision to leave the stop sign and proceed along the route. AI-based tools can provide probabilities, but these have to be linked to applicable models that help determine an action.

The organization may not believe that the financial and resource investment in AI tools is worth the benefit. In fact, some organizations are likely to implement a cheaper version that is far less effective. This could go horribly wrong. Possible problems in implementation and the inability to use AI results successfully include insufficient data, bad data, bad model development, poor logic-based interfaces, corrupt databases, lack of feedback, improper interpretation of results, and misunderstanding of model reliability. There is also a potential to use streaming data, which updates the AI algorithms for every instance a data point is captured. However, this can lead to instability because single data points are often variable and not representative of what might be captured in the future. Think back to a normal distribution in which you need to know the average value. Data points are scattered around the average, and the first data point might be one that is far from the average and therefore leads to an incorrect assumption about the pattern of the data. There could be an entire discussion about the frequency of data updates and the timing of executing software programs. For now, it is enough to know that there is no perfect answer.

If the organization is committed to standards of AI, they need to put an audit process in place. Failure to pass the audit can stall or delay implementation of the project. If a manager misuses the results, which subsequently leads to deterioration in an employee's mental health, the organization can face serious consequences, including legal action. If AI is misused when trying to optimize workplace productivity, serious mental and physical health issues are distinct possibilities. How easy is it to misuse AI? Think about NLP trying to understand a variety of accents, dialects, and phrases and misunderstanding them. The result can be the creation of an incorrect or skewed profile of a person and their work performance. This can result in replacing a worker with another person due to lower productivity, without understanding the causal correlation.

Another risk with machine learning algorithms is when they optimize one solution over another. This is known as runaway code. The example used by Nick Bostrom in his book *Superintelligence* is about using a machine learning algorithm to optimize the production of paperclips. The AI tool has a clear objective: to produce paper clips and to increase efficiency. In Bostrom's scenario, the machine learning tool optimizes production in a way that produces negative results in another area. For example, it takes over the capacity of the equipment used to produce staplers, which results in staplers not achieving their production objectives. For organizations trying to optimize productivity, they can face the risk that the actions taken regarding one employee have a negative impact on another employee. There should be restrictions in place in case the machine learning algorithm determines that requiring an employee to work a twenty-hour day on a task is more efficient. AI tools have objectives, but they also need boundaries, and these boundaries need to be clearly defined. Perhaps an algorithm will optimize productivity over other considerations, such as the environment or a person's mental or physical health. The concept of AI safety is fairly new, and safeguards must be put in place that protect the well-being of employees as well as the internal and external environment.

HOW DATA CAUSES UNRELIABLE OUTCOMES

Companies such as Facebook and Google understand the value of data, and they use it to create personalized marketing profiles to provide relevant ads. When building an accurate personal profile, the importance of structured data cannot be understated. Structured data is data that is in a standard format and easily accessible. Data is required to train the machine learning model, and most organizations do not manage data very well. Roughly 80 percent of the time spent in the process of creating a machine learning algorithm is committed to data, so it is clearly an essential step.[39] For most organizations, data is not clean. Data fields contain typos or improperly capitalized words. There are a variety of formats, the data fields do not have a clear meaning, and the contents do not follow a consistent format. Field formats are different across or sometimes within the same database. For example, a date field can be dd/mm/yy, mm/dd/yy, mm/week, yyyy/mm/dd, or any other possible permutation. There can be two data fields that actually mean the same thing and one data field that has two meanings. Understanding the important role of data helps us determine the most interesting and effective ways to reduce the accuracy of our profile. Alternately, it also helps us deliberately create a superlative profile.

AI algorithms are reliant on structured data, and even with consistent data, some calculations are not possible. For example, software code cannot add two data fields that contain zip codes and have a meaningful result. Blank data fields are a problem for AI, which is why if you fill out an online form, the required data fields are highlighted. Instead of leaving them blank, you can put nonsense in certain boxes. Sometimes when compelled to complete a text field to gain access to a website, I enter a few meaningless characters.

---

39   Gil Press, "Cleaning Big Data: Most Time-Consuming, Least Enjoyable Data Science Task, Survey Says," Forbes, March 23, 2016, https://www.forbes.com/sites/gilpress/2016/03/23/data-preparation-most-time-consuming-least-enjoyable-data-science-task-survey-says/#1ec00896f63.

CORRUPTION BY NATURAL CAUSES

In the book *Weapons of Math Destruction*,[40] Cathy O'Neil outlines the requirement for a feedback loop. In her judgment there needs to be an ongoing input of fresh data that supports the algorithm training process in order to maintain accurate results. There is no guarantee that an organization will follow this advice. Due to laziness or budget concerns, an organization may simply continue with the tools because they work, not realizing that over time, the accuracy degrades without fresh data. Maintaining and managing data is a lot of work and will be a good target for reducing the amount of effort as a way to save costs. Important to the maintenance of machine learning tools are regular software and data updates to ensure that the tools continue to produce accurate outcomes.

Businesses need to constantly update their processes to match the pace of technology change as well as other competitive pressures. This is the reason why machine learning tools are so important. Instead of constantly changing a process or updating software code, the machine learning tool uses the most recent data to make a decision. As the environment changes, so does the data, which means decisions or processes are always based on new data.

In addition, the resources to support this type of implementation on an ongoing basis are limited. AI experts and data scientists are growing in demand, and there is already a significant shortage of these resources.[41] Becoming a data scientist and learning new programming languages is not a simple process where existing workers can be easily converted. AI models require interpretation and knowledge of math and statistics. The purpose of these facts is to highlight that a machine

---

40 Cathy O'Neil, Weapons of Math Destruction: How Big Data Increases Inequality and Threatens Democracy (New York, NY: Penguin Books, 2016).

41 Brian Holak, "Demand for Data Scientists is Booming and Will Only Increase," Business Analytics, Jan 31, 2019, https://searchbusinessanalytics.techtarget.com/feature/Demand-for-data-scientists-is-booming-and-will-increase.

learning program might become less usable over time simply because there are no resources to support it. Performing support work is never as exciting as building new programs, which is where the limited resources are most likely to be deployed in the industry.

SUMMARY

While we attempt to increase our knowledge of how to deceive the AI-based tools, there is a possibility that the value of the software programs will deteriorate on their own. Implementation is fraught with pitfalls, as in any new technology or software deployment. The outcomes can be unreliable, or the results can be misinterpreted. In addition to all this, there needs to be constant update and maintenance. These are beneficial characteristics that help support our plan of deception, especially if our strategy reduces the reliability of the results, contributing to frustration and skepticism that the AI-based tools can be effective for the organization.

CHAPTER 16

AI under Attack

The possibility of sabotage to an AI data model is receiving increasing attention and has been termed "data poisoning."[42] This is defined as an attempt by an individual to inject bad data into a dataset used by a machine learning program so that it will lead to incorrect results. This is not the only threat to AI models that needs to be addressed by an organization. In addition to attacks that threaten the integrity of the data, there are attacks that can be made on the algorithms and the models themselves.

It should be noted that, similar to a lot of technology development, the ability to prevent these attacks typically lags behind adoption and use. With online security, new technology and tools to counter the invasion are frequently only implemented after a major privacy breach occurs and is publicized. It is not surprising that organizations also lag behind in understanding and adapting to data poisoning attacks. The

---

42 Ilja Moisejevs, "Poisoning Attacks on Machine Learning," Medium (Towards Data Science, July 14, 2019), https://towardsdatascience.com/poisoning-attacks-on-machine-learning-1ff247c254db.

cost and complexity to manage this phenomenon only exacerbates the problem and is likely to delay the ability to incorporate any kind of feasible solution.

An organization can simply ignore the problem and believe that the existing IT infrastructure is capable of preventing and repelling the attacks. Alternately, the organization might be committed to a business case approach and only seek to address any potential issues if it can be shown to be of greater value than the cost of the effort to increase data security. The cost might be determined as too high to acquire additional defenses for a problem that does not exist. The reality is that the problem might exist and be undetected, or it might not exist yet and will soon become evident. Finally, there is always the argument when purchasing software that it is a vendor's responsibility to build in safeguards to prevent attacks. Some organizations will be serious about this issue, while others will be naive.

ATTACKING THE DATA

An attack can be implemented from within the organization by accessing the training datasets for an AI algorithm and adding erroneous data. The tampered data pollutes the correlation that determines a probability model and results in an incorrect prediction value. If the poisoning is successful, the AI program may do something such as see an image of a kitten and classify it as a puppy. Data scientists who study image recognition believe that it only takes a small change to cause a bad classification.[43] This gives great hope to employees who are trying to deceive the AI models that create personal psychological profiles.

The consequences of inaccurate data fed to a machine learning model or attacks on the data can be significant. Let's say that the

---

43 BBC News, "AI Image Recognition Fooled by Single Pixel Change," BBC News (BBC, November 3, 2017), https://www.bbc.com/news/technology-41845878.

prediction model indicates a 95 percent probability of success, and that is an acceptable level for making subsequent decisions. Corrupt data is then inserted, leading to a 65 percent probability of success. Is a probability of 65 percent accuracy good enough? Not likely. Inserting corrupt data will lower the probability to an unacceptable level for taking action. With bad data, the prediction probability drops, and the organization needs to decide whether the level of probability is acceptable. By using bad data, a model can quickly lose credibility.

Feeding bad training data to the AI classifier commonly results in skewing the results of the model, which means a distortion in the ability to achieve a reliable correlation. The classifier no longer understands the difference between good data and bad data, and the correlation calculation results in a model can shift to favor the bad data. When you supply inaccurate historical data, it is referred to as targeting the model's integrity. One academic article reported that even under strong defenses, a 3 percent training dataset poisoning leads to an 11 percent drop in accuracy.[44]

In addition to data poisoning, there are a number of other concerns with datasets that are used to train machine learning models. A term known as *adversarial inputs* is the possibility that the data provided has a high probability of being misclassified. This type of misdirection is based on methods similar to those used to evade spam filters or antivirus detection. The goal in trying to corrupt machine learning models that create personal profiles is to provide data that sneaks into a dataset as acceptable and subsequently reduces the reliability of the results. Corrupt datasets can also be inadvertently supplied by vendors. As part of the initial training for a model, vendors can create training datasets,

---

44 Jacob Steinhardt, Pang Wei Koh, and Percy Liang, "Certified Defenses for Data Poisoning Attacks," arXiv.org (Cornell University, November 24, 2017), https://arxiv.org/abs/1706.03691.

and attackers may realize that altering these datasets is an easier path than attacking an existing machine learning model.

A lot of data is gathered from social media sites and other supposedly private websites. These sites are more susceptible to erroneous data and manipulation. At least, when it comes to social media, all the data is supplied by you, and you have the power to provide as little or as much data you want. To protect your own data privacy, you could also rationalize providing corrupt data, or at least inconsistent data, that is then scraped from social media sites by data brokers. This, of course, is different from the workplace where the organization can claim to own or at least be responsible for the data produced, and you are forced to give away your data in return for being employed.

The best defense against this type of deception starts with data cleansing, and even experts reveal this to be a time-consuming and thankless task. It takes time and effort to find outliers that really do not belong in the dataset, and even then, a data scientist might assign a probability that the outlier is actually real data. Failing to do so might lead to missing an eventual trend in the data. The inevitable conclusion for an employee is that inserting bad data into a dataset is worthwhile for deception because it can be very difficult to find, segregate, and remove. New strategies being proposed to prevent corruption in the data pipeline involve certifying training datasets, adding data encryption, and using the latest database technology to store metadata. New information technology software can alert an organization when there is an infiltration attempt, but it will not prevent individuals from providing their own misleading data that is captured as part of an ongoing employee monitoring process.

Another concern, as previously mentioned, is that AI models need to be constantly updated with recent data in order to remain accurate. The problem is that a model will lag a trend. Here is why this happens. Assume the data contains one outlier. The model will ignore it and retain the existing model. As time passes a second outlier occurs.

Once again, the model ignores it because it does not fit the correlation curve and is not statistically significant. Next, there is another outlier of the same value, and then another outlier follows. Now the model has to consider the outliers, and they are included in the model. At some point the model readjusts, and the outliers become part of the model. However, the model did not see the trend because the outliers did not form a pattern that could be included in the correlation until there were sufficient data points. AI algorithms are slow to adjust to trends. Similarly, AI algorithms will be slow to recognize data poisoning, possibly until it is too late, and the entire dataset must be ignored.

One of the ways to corrupt the model building process is known as *feedback weaponization*, which is the attempt to corrupt the model directly by ensuring the supervised learning or reinforcement learning is incorrect for a number of datasets. It misrepresents the data in the feedback loop by misclassifying the supervised learning labels for a training dataset. It is easier to falsify labels than to change dataset entries. Instead of each dataset having an accurate label, these can be randomly mixed or set to the same label for every instance. It can take place as part of a training pool, and this mixed data can be used to build a new model. This is one of the best possibilities for reducing model reliability. The advantage is that only a limited amount of data needs to be manipulated. The disadvantage is there is an uncertainty of knowing whether the result will be successfully disrupted. This assumes that you gain access to a dataset and understand the supervised learning approach used by machine learning algorithms.

ATTACKING THE MODEL

Model stealing is a technique where the originator replicates the existing model. This is done to find the best way to either counteract the model's effectiveness or improve on the model so that the new model becomes significantly more efficient. For personal profiles, this is a lot of work. However, if you create a parallel model, then it can be easily manipulated with different datasets. In fact, this is an ideal solution for knowing exactly what data is required as input to the model that will create a specific result. Model stealing is a way to know exactly what data should be fed to the real model in order to obtain the results that are desired.

Backdoor attacks seek to alter the software code.[45] They are malicious and illegal, and those who do this are usually detected and caught. A backdoor is access to the programming code that the model's designer is not aware of, but that the attacker can use to alter the machine learning outcomes. An attack might teach the classifier that a specific string of data or a behavior is benign. The attack might add a virus to the algorithm that can be triggered to falsify or ignore certain data and create an inaccurate output. Alternately, it could allow a model to be created but could have a very low reliability factor. These are much more sophisticated attacks and require knowledge and previous experience in this field. Direct changes to the machine learning code might not have a large impact on the result. Someone may try to manipulate hyperparameters, set the neural networks layers to 1, or change the number of iterations, known as epochs, to a much lower number. All of these are attempts to prevent the algorithm from training properly or arrive at a classification that has very low reliability.

SUMMARY

As machine learning algorithms become more popular, so will attacks that attempt to reduce their accuracy. It is more likely to happen first in the general marketplace and then become more common with AI

---

45 Tianyu Gu et al., "BadNets: Evaluating Backdooring Attacks on Deep Neural Networks," *IEEE Access* 7 (2019): pp. 47230–47244, https://doi.org/10.1109/access.2019.2909068.

software deployed in the workplace. The marketplace depends on pro-files to accelerate financial gain, such as online tracking or points cards for shoppers. For employers using AI tools, the solutions to prevent data attacks are likely to be available much later. Manipulating data and corrupting dataset labels are the easiest methods to reduce model reliability. For employees, it is important to be careful with your decep-tion and be knowledgeable about updates to the technology.

CHAPTER 17

AI Issues in the Workplace

AI tools will become more integrated into everything we do as humans, both at work and in our social lives, so there is increasing concern regarding data security and the privacy of our personal information. As AI tools are introduced into the workplace, the organization has a responsibility for the security of the data as well as for protecting personal privacy rights based on how the data is used. The problem is that the technology is new, so it is difficult to know what approach will work best. There are ethical considerations as well as potential legal liability for failure to manage these concerns properly. People have a right to know what procedures are in place to secure their data and how any data collected is being used. Will organizations be open to personal requests, or will audits be required as part of an industry or regulatory standard? Some employees might view intensive monitoring in the workplace as intrusive, and if actions are taken based on an ill-conceived model, there is justification for legal action against the organization.

ETHICS

Ethics is a significant concern that covers many areas. One problem is with extremely biased AI tools that, based on data, perform unintended profiling of individuals. In other words, there is a bias in historical data toward stereotypes. This might include women not becoming corporate executives or overrepresentation of minorities in prisons. Historical data includes activities that may no longer be deemed as appropriate in a modern society. As humans, most of us understand the need to progress and to become inclusive, because that is really what makes us human—the ability to be kind, forgiving, and welcoming. AI tools that use historical data have the ability to include prejudicial judgments and to use them in decision-making. We must identify and eliminate that hidden bias in data that is used by machine learning algorithms in order to move forward in a professional and human way.

Similarly, we need to avoid historical bias in personal information that is collected by the organization. For example, if a person had an addiction problem and is fully recovered, it should not be included in the data for an AI algorithm. Will a single bad event or circumstance create ongoing historical bias for an individual? A person might commit vandalism or shoplifting as a minor and then never be able to overcome the negative judgment from an AI tool. It is unfair, but AI only uses the data available. Nonetheless, organizations will rely on machine learning algorithms for making decisions. Employees and potential employees for an organization need to do everything possible to hide past events from being included in the data. Perhaps you change your looks or transpose your first and middle names to distance yourself from the negative data. A single past event should not be used to judge your current capabilities, but that is exactly what AI tools are likely to do.

Researchers and technology implementers are encouraged to join the FATE (fairness, accountability, transparency, and ethics) movement to provide some level of responsibility for developing and using AI in a way that is not harmful to humans. This is an approach supported by Microsoft. Google initiated a different approach by creating an external AI ethics board to oversee responsible development of AI at Google. Progress was limited, so the board was disbanded, and new efforts are underway.[46] The European Union published ethical guidelines for trustworthy AI, proclaiming that AI development should result in a product that is lawful, ethical, and robust. The term *robust* is interpreted to mean that it should function properly when deployed but should also meet the ethical and lawful criteria as time passes and as more data is added, especially from the social environment. The guidelines include seven more clearly defined requirements, such as privacy, data protection, and fairness in that AI systems should be accessible to all.[47] While these movements are encouraging, they are only indicators that a unified global agreement on ethical AI development will be extremely difficult, if not impossible, to achieve.

The initiatives so far are scattered, and there is no standard that can be incorporated into the organization's policies, so for now organizations need to be aware and implement their own standards to ensure that AI is used ethically. This will be a large and thankless responsibility, although at some point in the future, the value of this responsibility will become clear when an organization manages to avoid a significant ethical mistake that might have become newsworthy and resulted in massive negative consequences.

Another ethical issue is how AI tools assess employee performance. Current tools analyze how efficient team members are at completing a task and then may recommend a replacement based on habitually slower work. Is that fair? What exactly is affecting the individual's

---

46 Kelsey Piper, "Exclusive: Google Cancels AI Ethics Board in Response to Outcry," Vox (Vox, April 4, 2019), http://www.vox.com/future-perfect/2019/4/4/18295933/google-cancels-ai-ethics-board.

47 European Commission, "Ethics Guidelines for Trustworthy AI," Shaping Europe's digital future—European Commission, July 9, 2020, https://ec.europa.eu/digital-single-market/en/news/ethics-guidelines-trustworthy-ai.

work habits? Perhaps this day is an irregularity in their normal energy level. When an analytics tool determines that the individual needs to be replaced, what is the level of inefficiency, and how is that calculated? Allowing AI tools to use data is expected, but considerations must be taken regarding the nature of data used, especially when it results in negative consequences for employees. There also must be a policy on how much of an employee's digital footprint is retained and used. There needs to be a process to manage performance issues and should not involve data that is originally collected for AI tools and then diverted for another purpose.

A controversial area will be the collection of verbal and written communication to build a personality profile or to identify personal psychological characteristics. This is currently gathered for marketing purposes with our internet clicks. It can be collected in a workplace, but the danger occurs when it is used for manipulative purposes or provided without permission to a third party. In all cases, the use of personal data must be communicated clearly and in advance to those involved. The organization is ultimately responsible for these policies and decisions, and they must find a way to ensure that data is not used in an unprofessional manner.

People are reliant on the organization to protect their privacy and not mishandle or lose it in some negligent misadventure or breach of security. Security is a concern with data because data often represents the essence of the organization. For organizations that receive and utilize user data, there is an obligation to ensure that it is secure and not leaked to or breached by any unauthorized group. For AI, the data does not have to be "stolen" to build a successful model because the algorithm only needs to read the data to create a model. This adds a new level of concern for data. Will an intruder be able to access the data, read it, and then leave it as if no intrusion ever occurred? As detecting data breaches become more difficult, this makes it even more important to protect an organization's data.

FREEDOM OF PERSONAL INFORMATION

Can you ask to see the model that has been created that represents your personal profile? In consideration of the freedom of information rights, employers often allow employees to review their file, which is stored as part of the policy on managing human resources. There will be uncertainty if this also includes a model created by a machine learning algorithm. What might be offered is the algorithm and the database that created your profile, both of which will be difficult to analyze. Understanding a machine learning model will be a challenge. The correlations created by an algorithm, such as a neural network, will be nearly impossible to determine. A profile contains personality traits and collected performance data, so it might be easier to review the data than trying to understand the model-creation process. Assuming the data can be reasonably evaluated, the plan is to search for data that would create a noncausal correlation—in other words, are there any data points collected that have completely no relevance to a personal performance profile? The data probably includes the completion of assigned tasks, all communication sent or received in the workplace, as well as data captured that originated outside the workplace. There should also be an amount of irrelevant data. The next step is to check for a model that has low reliability score. Remember the issue of binary data, in which the result is 1 or 0? The result of 51 percent can be represented as a 1, which is very tenuous. How is the data used, and are actions taken on a probability score of 65 percent, for example?

Once you obtain your profile, you can compare this to a psychological model to gain a better understanding of how you are being profiled. This becomes a baseline for supplying outliers that do not match the model. It is also beneficial to know the advantages and drawbacks of the reference model being used. Not all models are worth using. Academic research is constantly evolving, so there needs to be caution in using outdated reference models. Similar to the premise that machine learning models need to be consistently updated with new data to stay accurate, any reference model also needs to be updated based on current development in psychological theory.

Once you discover some major flaws in your personal profile, you need to find a way to make changes. If you are not planning to use the information to provide outliers, the next step is to point out concerns to your employer. This can be effective if you have a good grasp of the math and can produce a logical argument that is based on data and supported by good concepts. For example, using binary numbers instead of probability values is a valid concern that should be addressed and resolved. A 65 percent probability will result in a 1, because it is over 50 percent, and will require action to be taken. But the value of 65 percent is actually quite far from being an accurate representation of the results. On the other hand, it is tougher to illustrate the flaws in a machine learning algorithm. It is difficult to argue that the model does not have the correct hyperparameters to create a valid correlation. That is beyond the grasp of most people, and it also is highly debated by AI practitioners. The model is based on data that is used as input to a computer system, so that is the best place to begin. Inaccurate or inappropriate input data can be disputed. You can also dispute the reliability of the results since it is unlikely that any model will achieve above 97 percent accuracy. Can you use that 3 percent difference from a perfect probability score to argue that the model is incorrect for your profile? Perhaps there is a set of conditions that makes the 3 percent much higher, and the data collection does not include those conditions. Since the model is based on data, it is your goal to find the erroneous data and feed the model the data that you want it to have.

AUDIT

Someone needs to ensure that AI systems conform to standard practices and meet employee and societal expectations, especially in terms of ethics and privacy. As an employee, it is wise to ask what policies and procedures are in place to audit algorithms, or if the organization abides by any of the standards of ethics applied to AI. The creation of an ethical process for collection and use of our personal data is a critical step in building credibility with employees. The policy needs to be easy to understand, and compliance needs to be verified on a regular basis. It is unlikely that a single policy can be used by all or even most employers. Each organization or industry may seek to utilize their AI tools for different purposes or for different levels of analysis and action.

An audit of AI algorithms includes whether they have implemented industry standards or adhere to the organization's own policies and procedures. For individuals, an audit must reveal the level of probability for a prediction that is being used to develop actions. What probability value drives an action or a decision? A 98 percent probability seems reasonable, and there will be a scale from 50 percent to 98 percent where actions may or may not be generated. This is something that needs to be determined and monitored. It can also provide feedback on how outliers are managed, something useful in our plan to deceive these tools.

Another issue is what your employer plans to do with your personal data once you leave the organization. You should be able to ask for your data or find a way to acquire proof that your data history has been erased. Even this will be controversial because any group activities that contain your data are unlikely to be separated and removed. It may require a third party to verify the removal of your data. Removal is not the same as data being archived. Organizations prefer to archive data in the event of a financial or legal issue that might arise in the future. The point here is another aspect of who owns your data. You also need to prevent them from continuing to use it or transfer it to other subsidiaries or contractors, even when a contract agreement is in place. This is the nightmare: you lose your data because one organization passes it on and now has no control over retrieving it.

There are several AI initiatives underway to ensure ethical use and control of the information and algorithms. Employees need to ask the organization what process they have in place and what standards they follow. This has a double benefit, and the first is that you should be reassured that the organization has standards. It also means that you may gain more insight into how to manage or deceive the model better. If the organization has no standards for managing the AI-based systems, that can be a problem that needs to be raised gently with senior members of the organization. It also means that there is a greater likelihood that the process and outcomes are not reliable.

The implications are obvious. There needs to be a compromise or accommodation for how AI programs collect data and how it is applied to employees in the organization. The resulting policy should be communicated to all employees, and there needs to be a guarantee of compliance with the agreed-upon policy. If people believe that they are giving up too much personal information with only negative returns, then employee sentiment will deteriorate. Alternately, it may not be evident that sentiment has deteriorated if employees are successful at deception, which should be even more concerning to the organization.

SUMMARY

There are numerous ethical and data security issues that go beyond the creation of a personal psychological profile. Personal data is passed around by employers and provided to external entities, usually under an agreement that an employee can barely understand. Employees need to hold the organization accountable for the security of personal data and question the policies under which AI tools are introduced and used.

If you have the ability to view the components that are used to create your profile, there are ways to respond that might improve your ability to deceive or your ability to question how the organization is using your data. This is another opportunity to resist the effort to dominate you with customized influence capability and make you conform to the organization's goals.

There are no generally accepted industry standards for fair use of AI tools. Audits need to be mandatory moving forward. This field is relatively new, and it will be the employee's responsibility to uncover the audit practices of the organization and how serious concerns, such as historical bias in the data, are being managed. These questions can be asked without requiring in-depth technical knowledge. The responsibility is clearly on the organization to provide data security and ethical use of the data. Both of these must be clearly explained and properly monitored.

CHAPTER 18

Additional Technology in the Workplace

A I is not the only technology that will have an impact on the workplace. Other tools based on evolving technologies will change what employees do and how they perform their assigned tasks. Some tools will link into AI or have AI in the background, while others will be implemented without AI and provide a function for a designated purpose. A brief overview of some new technologies is included next.

INTERNET OF THINGS

The internet of things (IoT) uses cameras and smart devices to capture data and feed it to a system that can make decisions. If it is included in a refrigerator door, it can scan the contents, realize you have no milk, and add it to your shopping list or even add it to a list of food that can be subsequently ordered automatically. In the workplace, the addition of IoT devices provides the opportunity to capture more data because IoT is a natural data collection technology. The cost of these devices has decreased dramatically, which means their availability and usage has significantly increased. IoT devices include sensors that can be embedded in equipment, medical devices, and even people. The example mentioned earlier in the book was employees having a chip inserted under their skin, used to open security doors. Sensors can be used to detect changes in temperature, movement, and other conditions. As the vendors of workplace surveillance software become more creative, expect to find at least hundreds of these devices deployed throughout a work environment. This series of networked devices will identify you in a variety of settings and gather data points as you go about your work activities as well as your life.

BEACON TECHNOLOGY

The marketplace also has a new technology for in-store shopping, called beacon technology. Beacons access smartphone apps and perform two main functions. They collect data and target customers with ads for specific purchases. Data collected includes tracking the customer's movement around the store as well as providing a location function to make it easier to find items on a shopping list. In an attempt to increase in-store purchases, beacon technology is used to send shoppers discounts and alerts for sales, especially when they are standing near the items being advertised. Organizations will soon adopt this technology for employees. Alerts can be sent when work priorities change, and locating an employee inside a workplace becomes much easier. Alerts in the form of gentle reminders are also easily implemented for employees who take excessive time during breaks or lunch. Beacon technology can become the new one-way communication tool that combines with psychological profiles to send the perfect motivational message at the perfect time.

ROBOTIC PROCESS AUTOMATION

RPA is the acronym for Robotic Process Automation. This is the ability to take repetitive tasks and automate them into a software program. It has become increasingly popular with the implementation of chatbots for customer service requests. It is also used with NLP to interpret incoming emails and take an action, such as adding a meeting or reminder to a person's calendar. RPA takes existing tasks and uses software logic to automate the sequence of tasks in a process. In many situations, this is a terrible idea. If you have a bad or poorly performing process, the worst action is to automate that bad process. Yet many organizations become enamored with the technology and forget their purpose is to provide value. RPA is similar to the machine learning concept in that the process needs to be updated, or it will become less reliable. Machine learning needs to be updated with more recent data in order to remain accurate. RPA will become dominant in the workplace for organizing meetings and creating a summary or status report of recent activities. It can also be used to automate the collection of data for each employee.

Once known simply as "automation," RPA is becoming more technologically advanced. It threatened to wipe out factory jobs, and now it is being used for office and computer-based work. Automation using robots is a fairly common technology. RPA is interesting in that repetitive work is always a prime target for automation and as RPA evolves, more complex tasks will be automated. This is an important development for workplaces that have some variability in completing tasks and less repetitive tasks. RPA, combined with machine learning, will be able to adjust as changes are made and eventually even predict them. With AI, robots can be augmented with machine learning algorithms that make them capable of making decisions based on data. Your personal productivity in the workplace will depend on providing value beyond what can be performed by automation and will be based on a series of interactive tasks.

BLOCKCHAIN

Blockchain is a type of distributed database that secures records in a unique way that makes them difficult to alter. It was developed to serve the needs of the cryptocurrency, bitcoin, and it has been adopted by other fields that require secure data and secure data transactions, such as in the financial and legal fields. This has currently little to no impact on employee surveillance and profiling, but it might eventually be a possibility for securing personal data collection. Since it is encrypted, this database provides the organization more security and makes the data less vulnerable to rogue attacks.

SUMMARY

Technology development is continuous, and it will be important to understand the implications for workplace data collection. This is not meant to be an extensive list. More visible developments, such as self-driving vehicles, are a combination of existing technologies. The development of new technologies is ongoing, and some of the development will become a concern for workplace surveillance and employee profiling. As more technology is deployed both inside and outside the workplace, every step, gesture, word, and tone become collectible data points. As you build your good deception habits, the changes should only have a minimal impact. However, it is likely that tracking will be more meticulous and more invasive to your work and personal life.

CHAPTER 19

The Future of AI Tools in the Workplace

The AI tools being used now are based on concepts developed several years ago. We can easily extrapolate that the next generation of AI tools will be more powerful and better predictors of human behavior. Image capture and analysis of emotional expression will be faster and more accurate. Human behavior analysis software will seem as if it reaches inside our minds and extracts our thoughts. It will also extract our mood and understand the most convincing way to communicate with us to evoke the desired response.

Imagine you are in a small room and that you're being analyzed by an experienced professional psychologist. I once knew a woman who was very skilled at psychology. Based on her interaction with a person, she could precisely determine the probability of their future behavior. She used Rorschach (inkblot) tests to evaluate inmates in correctional institutions to determine if they were a risk to reoffend. As obscure as this might seem, she had an incredible prediction success rate of well over 90 percent. Now imagine that there are one hundred people like her, fully trained and experienced psychologists, analyzing your every action and emotional state. That is the next generation of AI that will be used in the workplace. The analysis will be far more accurate, and the ability to predict and direct our behavior will be frightening.

Next-generation AI is at its scariest when AI algorithms perform analysis instantly based on our current situation, taking into account our behavior, personality, and emotional state. The AI tools can predict what we are going to do or say next. The AI tools will know what to communicate and how we are most likely to react. This is the ultimate ability to manipulate our work life and constrain our free will. The AI tools of the future will know how to motivate us to be more creative as well as more productive. They will direct us to conform, meaning that we will become the person that the organization wants us to be and do what the organization wants us to accomplish. They will know what is needed to compel us to continue to be highly productive at work with the existing organization or to become unhappy with our work assignments and leave. This becomes the most effective human resources management process possible.

INCREASING DATA COLLECTION

It is the era of data collection, and organizations are determined to gather massive amounts of data about us. In the book *The Autonomous Revolution*, the intensive data collection about consumers is called *the surveillance economy*, in which data is monitored or collected for every consumer action.[48] At some point, organizations realized that making decisions based on data is immensely more likely to result in a successful outcome than an unsuccessful one.

---

48   William H. Davidow, Michael S. Malone, *The Autonomous Revolution: Reclaiming the Future We've Sold to Machines*, Berrett-Koehler Publishers, Oakland, February 18, 2020.

Data is rapidly collected on us every day. For example, I drive to the store using a navigation app to provide directions. The app collects my starting point, which is most likely my residence, the destination, and how long it takes me to arrive. The duration can be compared to traffic and stops along the way and determine if I am a fast driver or slow driver, or if I obey the speed limit with a passion. At my destination, which is a grocery store, I fill up my cart and proceed to the checkout. I offer my shopping points card to build up an incredibly miniscule number of redeemable points, and the store adds all my purchases to a database. I pay for the groceries with my credit card, and the bank collects the time, date, value of my purchase, and location. I make another stop and use a different card to collect air miles points. A different organization collects that data, although it might be consolidated if the two stores are actually part of the same conglomerate. The data collection process is similar in the workplace, but the analysis and interpretation of the data will be far more insightful and accurate with future machine learning tools. More underlying patterns will be exposed, possibly ones that we are not even aware of ourselves. Trends will be detected more easily and compared to our personal psychology.

Collecting data will intensify because, as we know, AI-based algorithms are sponges for data. Data is more important than other parameters for producing an accurate result. Neural networks of the future will find a normalized state in which the layers and coding are standardized, programs become commodities, and the data is the most valuable component. In fact, the value of data will increase dramatically as people realize the many uses and potential for the results. If we are being bribed now to provide data, this will not only intensify but also become more subtle. Some people will simply surrender and accept that they cannot stop the data collection, while others will try to minimize or distort what is being collected.

In addition to a dramatic improvement in analysis, AI tools of the future will use more data and begin gathering it earlier. As children increasingly use technology and carry smartphones, they will be maneuvered into unwittingly providing even more data about themselves than adults. Data collected from games they play or online comments they make allow much earlier analysis and creation of a psychological profile. Similar to the movie *Divergent*, teenagers and young adults can then be streamed into an optimized career choice. Currently there are people who do not fit naturally into the field they want to have as a career, so they push themselves with extreme effort to develop those skills. They develop an ability to adapt and learn because they want to work in a field that needs them, or perhaps they simply admire the work. They achieve more personal development by taking a new path and being successful. The next generation of AI will not allow this. A person will be streamed into a field that is more compatible for them, and only students who are adept at learning a certain subject will be chosen to develop that skill. Although children will not be subject to workplace surveillance, their data will be accessed by employers through data brokers in order to assess their personality and ability to comply with organizational goals.

Young people are especially susceptible as targets for data collection. Apps offered by companies such as Facebook have a locator game. Based on the public information already available online, the Facebook app can locate and display exactly where a person's roommate lives. Many young people are perfectly comfortable sharing their data online. Before the digital age, they would have found it creepy for this amount of personal information to be available.

Apps like Google Maps show images of people mowing their front lawn, and Uber has a map that shows where their cars are. A black box can be added to a person's car to receive discounted rates on insurance for not speeding, another great example of bribing someone for sharing more data. There is a level of acceptance that makes the availability of data no longer disturbing.

Data collection capability will become far more sophisticated and definitely more insidious. Without your knowledge, algorithms will search and find a partner for you, then identify their personal interests and highlight what you have in common that can be leveraged to influence your behavior. This becomes matchmaking without the website and is another example of the drive toward conformity. It will be difficult to resist. In fact, advanced AI tools will survey all your social and workplace connections and find your psychological weakness in order to prey on you to make this happen.

Another development will be the further integration of AI-based tools for managing employees using technologies such as data mining and the internet of things (IoT). Data mining can be used to analyze data across an entire group of employees to find specific anomalies or correlate reasons for success. It can identify weaknesses in teamwork or team members and identify the team members who are the hidden reasons for superior results. IoT is the interrelated connection of computer-based sensors. Examples of video capture include cameras that document progress on a construction project, a web scraper that takes a snapshot of progress on a software deployment project, and a dash cam that tracks and records deliveries. Sensors are devices, usually connected wirelessly, embedded in items around the workplace, and placed at strategic locations in the environment. The myriad of available IoT devices will be deployed inside and outside the workplace to provide an enormous amount of useful data.

MORE EFFECTIVE ANALYSIS

The tools that appear to read our minds, identify our personal psychological profiles, and create motivational messages will be far advanced as well as hidden in the background of an IT infrastructure. Unless employees find a way to disrupt the sequence of creating and using personal profiles, the organization will capitalize on our psychological frailty to gain an overwhelming advantage.

Deceiving AI will be more difficult because your data will be more integrated across many activities. If you want to purchase an item, your credit score and propensity to return items will be checked. If you apply for college, your book purchase history and social media activity will be collected and analyzed. Organizations will increasingly share personal data with others under the guise of a third-party contract. How can we possibly face these insurmountable odds and retain our humanity? The first step is to understand the machine learning process itself. The tools are nothing more than mathematical equations based on calculus. Next, the single most important criterion for effective results is the collection of data. Once we understand the incredible significance of personal data, we can begin to effect change. We can make attempts to protect ourselves and, even more importantly, start at an earlier time period and protect our children. Data gathering in the near future will start much earlier and be much more extensive. It is easier to mold a child than an adult. We are entering a world where data models become our prison, and we need to find escape routes or avoid getting captured.

In spite of the perception promoted by this book that AI is incredibly invasive and manipulative, my prediction is that these tools will become accepted and common in the workplace. Most humans are kind and forgiving. We are swayed by arguments that we intrinsically want to believe in, and resistance is often a much tougher path. We can be easily convinced that our compensation and working at a desired employment choice surpasses any negative implications. Managers will become smooth sales professionals who understand how to use our psychological profiles and communicate extremely effectively to make us amenable to the organization's objectives. In fact, managing might not require humans. Imagine during your workday, a virtual assistant checks in on you with a cool, calm, and collected voice with tasks personalized to your work habits. You hear the words: "You're working really hard. It's time for a quick break" or a reminder such as "You're delivering a presentation on Tuesday morning; how are you feeling about that? Here are five quick tips for staying calm and giving *great* presentations." Managers of the future might be an AI voice similar to Alexa, Siri, or Google Assistant who analyze our data much more quickly and effectively. It is not that we are weak; we are just adaptable to trends and technology.

There are popular opposing viewpoints when it comes to the AI technology used to monitor and manage employees. This is similar to a sliding scale, which is shown in table 10. On the one end, they postulate that the impact of AI is benign and not worthy of further consideration. This viewpoint believes that there will be no ill effects and no conformity or manipulation. If the technology is used to generate motivational techniques, it will be to our benefit. This side assumes that we are still in control and can always say no and attempt to find work with a different organization. If AI-based manipulation is in place, the belief is that the impact will be insignificant on our choices and especially insignificant in our personal lives outside the workplace.

Table 10: Scale of Change

Benign							Apocalypse

The other end of the scale is a doomsday prediction of the complete annihilation of our ability to counter the impact of AI-based persuasiveness. The premise is that we will slowly lose our free will to make our own decisions under the overbearing manipulation delivered by advanced AI tools that know all the triggers in our personal psychology. The result is complete subjugation of workers who conform to the organization's goals with no consideration of their own. Their work life will be directed by organizational requirements. People can be valued or cast off as required, used like the ink in a disposable pen, and then thrown away if it is more efficient to acquire a new one.

The middle ground is one where the employee and an organization have equal power. This assumes that an employee recognizes the circumstances and has the ability to either accept the direction or make their own. It assumes that in some instances, the organization will dominate and in other situations the employee will have an advantage.

My view of this scale is that the reality is likely neither and both. I doubt it will fall somewhere in the middle because the technology is too powerful. Therefore, I believe that both diametric views will become reality. More specifically, where the technology is implemented well and managed successfully and with clear goals, the manipulation and conformity will be irresistible. This requires a clear strategy for acquisition of data, implementation of AI software programs, and development of training and utilization plans. These organizations understand how technology is used to drive increased economic value for the organization. Numerous organizations will also implement the technology poorly, mishandle data collection, ignore data updates, and mismanage the tools as well as the objectives of the organization. Maybe the organization has insufficient skills in the process of implementing new technology, or perhaps they are unable to align their organizational goals with how the technology can help. The result of this type of implementation will be benign and, in some situations, laughable.

For organizations that are effective at utilizing these tools, productivity will increase dramatically and provide a distinct competitive advantage. The problem will be finding a way to be continuously effective without sacrificing the other goals of the organization, such as maintaining high standards for health, safety, security, and ethical issues. This is the AI trade-off scenario, where one goal is achieved to the detriment of another. It happens when the vendor or software developer fails to create a solution that considers all requirements of the organization. As with any new technology, there will be unforeseen issues that need carefully considered resolutions. Decisions made at the initial stages tend to become standards or policies for the ongoing process of employee management, and a process needs to be in place to revisit or update those policies as the technology advances.

If an organization is unsuccessful using AI-based employee management tools, they will struggle to find other ways to improve employee productivity. In fact, some employees may choose to work at organizations that do not use AI-based technology to manage employees. Perhaps there are certain types of organizations that are a better fit for being able to implement and successfully use these tools, an assumption that is yet to be determined. However, it is likely that all organizations will eventually incorporate some form of AI-based human resources management in the future. As with most technologies, the software costs drop over time, and the tools will become much easier to implement and use.

The next generation of AI continues to be developed but requires time and imagination in order to be commercialized. Machine learning algorithms and NLP are not recent developments and the developments in AI over the past five years or more are only beginning to trickle into actionable tools. There are several technical concepts that will eventually find their way into software programs. Brief descriptions of these concepts are below.

Adversarial data is used in a machine learning program where corrupt data is fed as training data, leading to incorrect results. Developers use this technique to discover weaknesses in the program and look for hidden bias in the data that might cause poor results. Algorithm auditing is also advancing in sophistication. This is a structured process, reviewing the software program design, algorithm coding, and datasets. The purpose is to uncover flaws, hidden biases, and how these can be resolved prior to making decisions based on the results.

Greater developments are underway in the area of emotional AI. Based on patterns in text, voice, and facial expressions, the AI systems are trained to recognize human emotions. This is useful for detecting stress and reacting appropriately or detecting when a person is being untruthful for personal gain. When the interaction is with a chatbot, the AI system responds accordingly by simulating human emotions in the way it communicates a response. Deep learning networks are being developed for greater analysis of human feelings, which will improve the accuracy of creating effective responses.

Another concept is to use genetic algorithms in combination with machine learning code to improve the results. The development of genetic algorithms is inspired by Charles Darwin's theory of natural evolution. Like the theory of evolution, the programming code finds a way to evolve toward the best fit or most adaptable solution. This is useful for very difficult problems that have many possible solutions. It begins with an iterative approach, similar to neural networks, and uses the concept of mutation and selection to find an optimized solution. The important technique incorporated in this type of software program is a fitness evaluation that is included in the code to provide feedback on the better of two or more options. This is used to evolve the iterations to find the best solution.

The most intriguing area of research is with teaching an AI system common sense. AI does not know if a bicycle is alive. AI does not know that a wall made of hanging fabric can be moved aside. These are simple for humans to understand, yet AI cannot comprehend abstract situations or problems and display good judgment.[49] To solve this, development is starting to focus on unsupervised learning and reinforcement learning concepts. It is an attempt to build a machine learning system that resembles the knowledge of a child and finds ways to train

---

49 Intel, "Neuromorphic Computing, Beyond Today's AI," Intel, 2020, https://www.intel.ca/content/www/ca/en/research/neuromorphic-computing.html.

it over time, similar to a child growing older. This concept is based on the work of Alan Turing, considered the father of computer science and artificial intelligence. In an article published in 1950, Alan Turing proposed the concept that a machine learning tool does not have to be a perfectly complete model as long as it can be taught how to learn.[50]

For any new concept, it takes clever and imaginative people to find ways to capitalize on the research. This technology will advance rapidly and become more invasive than anyone expects. The ethics and security guidelines around AI development will not prevent new tools from being implemented in the workplace. As long as we understand how these concepts are created, we have a chance to manage our own lives instead of having AI tools give us guidance that seems impossible to ignore.

As AI technology continues to advance, the implications for those employees who can deceive and control AI-based models is uncertain. Future AI technology has the potential for far greater accuracy and may not be as affected if we try to fool or direct the results. Data collection will be pervasive and timely, and the tools will be more intuitive at determining a human's emotional state. The best way to resist is to manage your data because all of these algorithms still rely on data. We might not be able to corrupt the algorithm, but we can control the data. We need to maintain our psychological integrity and always be aware that we have free will. Humans have natural defense mechanisms, and these help us survive. The best defense is to acknowledge and believe that AI tools are trying to manipulate us. We might need to second-guess every workplace communication without becoming too cynical.

It is also important to ask questions. You can question the reliability and then question the outcome. You can argue that certain data is

---

50   Alan Turing, "Computing Machinery and Intelligence," *Mind* 59, 236 (1950): 433–460, http://www.jstor.org/stable/2251299.

an exception and not part of the 95 percent probability. Perhaps the latest personal communication you received is based on a 65 percent probability of being the correct analysis. You can push back at the results produced because we know that any machine learning result has a probability factor.

Another strategy is using your own personal data points to collect and present your own profile. While an employer may have difficulty refuting this type of defense, it will require a group effort. Most individuals don't have the skills or sufficient comparative data to develop this on their own. Regardless, as technology advances, the ability to defend ourselves becomes more complex and less possible. We need to develop a basic knowledge of how the tools work and start the process of managing our data now, before it is too late.

SUMMARY

The next generation of AI tools will be more powerful and more insightful. The new techniques used to collect and analyze our data will be both creative and invasive. In the future, it may seem as if we are under a microscope, where every single movement, expression, communication, and action is captured and intensely analyzed. However, the tools will still be based on data, and it is our responsibility to manage the data they receive. If we recognize their blatant attempts as a manipulation of our behavior, we can use our free will to make our own decisions. This will be a difficult challenge when we are trying to counter the influence of a system that has in-depth knowledge of our psychological triggers and responses. This is especially more difficult when the data gathering and the analysis begin at a much younger age. We need to be self-aware and understand that free will is a way to randomize or control our behavior when a computer model is adept at predicting our behavior. The next generation of AI will truly know us better than we know ourselves. Will AI algorithms mold us into the workers that are most needed by the organization—or will we find our free will and make spontaneous decisions about our future? It's really up to you.

CHAPTER 20

Conclusion

Free will is about having a choice, and we need to exercise that choice in the face of AI-based tools that track our every step. Are we even capable of circumventing powerful AI psychological profiles that seek to direct our destiny? This is the era of data collection, and our environment is now a database. Every step we take, every word we say, and every behavior is being fed into a machine learning algorithm. In the workplace, we are forced to make keystrokes and reveal our locations, but we can fight back. We need to take control of our data and learn how to manage the outcomes of AI tools better than those who created them.

Employee monitoring software is already being used, and there are numerous blaring product ads for software attempting to ensnare businesses with promises of greater productivity. The pressures of a market economy dictate that increased productivity will always be a mandate. The challenges of competition and the obsession with economic gain continue to fuel the objective to increase productivity. That objective results in employees being the target for new tools in the workplace and vendors who encourage new methods to manage human resources. The only group not consulted in this productivity triangle are the employees. They become the victims of a technology that is based on probabilities.

As AI uses psychological tools in the workplace, a new disorder is likely to appear. Based on constant interactions that are specifically designed to influence an individual, an increased amount of stress can develop, which I call *profile anxiety*. This is my term for employees who understand that AI is creating a model based on data used to manage their actions in the workplace and determine their employment future. Profile anxiety is the fear of a personal model that is inaccurate, incomplete, or misused and results in detrimental consequences for an employee. It is unlikely that an employer will grant access to a person's model, and even if they do, it will be difficult to interpret the results. Workplace data, combined with personality traits, becomes an important psychological tool. The only way to change the model is to deliberately limit the amount of personal data, provide data outliers, and supply self-created specific data points. While this may sound lengthy, this process can help manage the data, especially if it is followed up by assessing results based on an employer's feedback.

If the content has left you confused, then think about some of the simple steps you can take. Although the statistical explanations are included in this book, it is only to provide background. Always remember that the major influence on any effort to categorize you is the data. Create a strategy for what you will share and how you plan to deceive the AI-based tools by limiting data, providing outliers, and creating your own data points. Think about a daily or weekly routine, and once you start, it will become a habit. Employer feedback can be used to adjust your strategy, if necessary. Keeping it simple and establishing new habits is the best way to start.

It will also be important to include the practice of deception in your personal life due to the long reach of workplace data collection tools. Creating a habit of using deception techniques in your personal life also helps to avoid the suppression of your free will against the power of AI-based marketing tools that convince you to make decisions based on understanding your personal profile. It is time to control and even repel the suggestive messages that attempt to wrap us in a cloak of conformity and direct our decisions.

When a writer says that AI can reach inside a person's head and read their mind, they are speaking metaphorically. AI tools need data points, and they cannot find them inside brain matter. Easily read data points are behaviors, facial expressions, and verbal or text communication. Massive amounts of personal data are collected, and the analysis is becoming faster and more accurate. The price of these workplace monitoring and profiling tools is rapidly decreasing, making them easily affordable and part of a sound business case, in which the costs are outweighed by the benefit of improved productivity.

This content is not meant to deny who you are or force you into always having to be careful about what you do. It is about finding a way to be exactly who you want to be and denying any AI algorithm from changing that. The suggestions included here are a template for finding ways to be yourself, in spite of new technology that tries to create a psychological profile, influence you in a manipulative way, and eventually take away your ability to be human. The ultimate goal is to prevent AI-based software from directing your work life so that you can make your own decisions and plan your own career. If we are not careful, these tools will stereotype us into a person who is unable to break away from that confinement and prevent us from exhibiting those abilities that make us human. Do not allow artificial intelligence to take away your ability to be who you are, the ability to make your own decisions, and most importantly, the ability to demonstrate your free will.

Acknowledgments: Paul Boudreau

This book evolved from content in a previous book that I wrote about AI and project management. The concept of project managers being tracked by an organization using AI-based tools cried out for more extensive research. AI is an evolving field and will result in some incredible benefits to the world. At the same time, people will find ways to use it, either intentionally or unintentionally, to produce negative consequences. I felt the need to reveal some of those negative possibilities.

Thanks once again to the amazing people I work with at Algonquin College in Ottawa, Canada. Thanks to my coauthor, Caitlin, who inspired me with new ideas and her youthful perspective that was critical to developing the content. Also, thanks once again to my wife, Jill, for her constant support and encouragement.

—Paul

Acknowledgments: Caitlin Schmidt

Thank you to Paul for his spectacular guidance and encouragement. His knowledge and expertise on AI tools are amazing, and none of this would have been possible without him. Although it is a technology still in its developing stages, I'm blown away as to how AI technology and machine learning have the power to effect revolutionary changes in the world.

A big thank-you to my parents and my brother, Emmerson, for their unwavering support. I am grateful for my mom, Wendy, for encouraging me to start writing. Thank you to Anik Singal and Jeremy Bellotti, who have both inspired me in countless, immeasurable ways. Finally, thank you to my partner, Carl, for his AI enthusiasm and encouragement. So thankful to have you in my life.

—Caitlin

About the Authors

Paul Boudreau, MBA, PMP, is a highly respected and influential management professional with over thirty-five years' experience in the technology industry. Paul is a professor at Algonquin College in Ottawa, Canada, where he teaches in the School of Business. He currently uses his knowledge of Python programming language and background in software applications to research and develop AI concepts. His most recent work is on machine learning and natural language-processing programs and how they are used in organizations.

Paul's first book, *Applying Artificial Intelligence to Project Management*, was well received for both professional and practical insights into a complex new technology. He followed up with his second book in this field, *How the Project Management Office Can Use Artificial Intelligence to Improve the Bottom Line*. Boudreau is known for presenting compelling arguments about how AI technology is changing the way organizations are managed and is increasingly being requested to speak at conferences.

Paul lives in Ottawa, Canada, where he pursues his lifelong ambitions to teach and write. He enjoys relaxing at his cottage with his wife, Jill, and their two dogs.

Caitlin Schmidt became fascinated by the field of artificial intelligence while studying law and human rights at Carleton University. As a facilitator at Carleton, Caitlin led workshops on human rights and digital privacy laws. Growing up in the digital age, she is particularly interested in the way that artificial intelligence is rapidly collecting our information and what this means for our future.

From Toronto, Ontario, Canada, Caitlin now lives in Ottawa, where she dedicates her time writing and creating videos. She enjoys dancing with her friends and family, and spending time with her cat, Mochi.

References

Access Now. "Human Rights in the Age of Artificial Intelligence."
   AccessNow.org. Access Now, 2018. https://www.accessnow.org/
   cms/assets/uploads/2018/11/AI-and-Human-Rights.pdf.

Affectiva. "Home." Affectiva, 2020. https://www.affectiva.com/.

Andre, Rae, and Peter D. Ward. 1984. *The 59-Second Employee: How to
   Stay One Second Ahead of Your One-Minute Manager*. Lincoln, NE:
   HarperCollins.

Armitage, Hanae. "X-ray Results Can Provide Higher Accuracy than
   a Trained Technician." Medical Xpress. November 2018. https://
   medicalxpress.com/news/2018-11-ai-outperformed-radiologists-
   screening-x-rays.html.

Barrett, Brian. "An Artist used 99 Phones to Fake a Google Maps
   Traffic Jam." Wired. February 3, 2020. https://www.wired.com/
   story/99-phones-fake-google-maps-traffic-jam/.

BBC News. "AI Image Recognition Fooled by Single Pixel Change."
   BBC News. BBC. November 3, 2017. https://www.bbc.com/news/
   technology-41845878.

Bennett, Chris, Tyson Gratton, and Jason Yao. "Website Cookies in Canada: Is Consent Required?" Lexology, April 2, 2020. https://www.lexology.com/library/detail. aspx?g=9a2dd4b7-bf75-4957-ac97-331ac98cebca.

Bertallee, Celina. "New Study: 64% of People Trust a Robot More Than Their Manager." Oracle. October 15, 2019. https://www.oracle. com/corporate/pressrelease/robots-at-work-101519.html.

Blanchard, Ken H., and Spencer Johnson. *The One Minute Manager*. United States: William Morrow & Co, 1982.

Boudreau, Paul. *How the Project Management Office Can Use Artificial Intelligence to Improve the Bottom Line*. New York: Elite Authors, 2020.

Dachis, Adam. "How Can I Tell If I'm Being Monitored at Work and What Can I Do About It?" Lifehacker. March 12, 2012. https://lifehacker.com/ how-can-i-tell-if-im-being-monitored-at-work-and-what-c-5894689.

Davidow, William H., and Michael S. Malone. 2020. *The Autonomous Revolution: Reclaiming the Future We've Sold to Machines*. Oakland, CA: Berrett-Koehler Publishers, Inc.

Deloitte. "Global Human Capital Trends: The Rise of the Social Enterprise." *Deloitte Insights*. 2020. https://www2.deloitte.com/ content/dam/insights/us/articles/HCTrends2018/2018-HCtrends_ Rise-of-the-social-enterprise.pdf.

European Commission. "Ethics Guidelines for Trustworthy AI." Shaping Europe's digital future. European Commission. July

9, 2020. https://ec.europa.eu/digital-single-market/en/news/ethics-guidelines-trustworthy-ai.

European Union. "Principles of the GDPR." European Commission—An official website of the European Union, June 7, 2019. https://ec.europa.eu/info/law/law-topic/data-protection/reform/rules-business-and-organisations/principles-gdpr_en.

Fingas, Jon. "Ultrasonic bracelet jams the microphones around you." Engadget. February 15, 2020. https://www.engadget.com/2020/02/15/ultrasonic-microphone-jamming-bracelet/.

Ford, Martin. "Yan LeCun." Essay. In *Architects of Intelligence: The Truth about AI from the People Building It*, 135. Birmingham, UK: Packt Publishing, 2018.

Gil Press. "Cleaning Big Data: Most Time-Consuming, Least Enjoyable Data Science Task, Survey Says." Forbes. March 23, 2016. https://www.forbes.com/sites/gilpress/2016/03/23/data-preparation-most-time-consuming-least-enjoyable-data-science-task-survey-says/#1ec00896f63.

Google. "Google Terms of Service—Privacy & Terms." Google. 2020. https://policies.google.com/terms.

Graham, Jefferson. "Don't Look Now, but Your Boss Is Probably Spying on Your Work Phone or Computer." USA Today. Gannett Satellite Information Network, October 9, 2019. https://www.usatoday.com/story/tech/2019/10/08/is-the-boss-tracking-you-now/3901594002/.

Gregory Richards. "Data Poisoning of AI Initiatives: What Is It and What to Do About It." Government Analytics Research Institute. February 2020 Issue. http://governmentanalytics.institute/magazine/february-2020/data-poisoning-of-ai-initiatives-what-is-it-and-what-to-do-about-it/.

Gu, Tianyu, Kang Liu, Brendan Dolan-Gavitt, and Siddharth Garg. "BadNets: Evaluating Backdooring Attacks on Deep Neural Networks." *IEEE Access* no.7 (2019): 47230–44. https://doi.org/10.1109/access.2019.2909068.

Hill, Kashmir. "The Secretive Company That Might End Privacy as We Know It." The New York Times, February 10, 2020. https://www.nytimes.com/2020/01/18/technology/clearview-privacy-facial-recognition.html.

Holak, Brian. "Demand for Data Scientists Is Booming and Will Only Increase." SearchBusinessAnalytics. TechTarget, January 31, 2019. https://searchbusinessanalytics.techtarget.com/feature/Demand-for-data-scientists-is-booming-and-will-increase.

Hubstaff. "Spend Less Time Tracking and More Time Growing." Hubstaff time tracker software. 2020. https://hubstaff.com/.

Intel. "Neuromorphic Computing, Beyond Today's AI." Intel. 2020. https://www.intel.ca/content/www/ca/en/research/neuromorphic-computing.html.

Interguard. "Employee Monitoring, Web Filtering, Productivity Tracking." InterGuard, June 17, 2020. https://www.interguardsoftware.com/.

Jagannathan, Meera. "These Are the Employees Most Likely to Cheat at Work." MarketWatch. November 17, 2017. https://www.marketwatch.com/story/these-are-the-employees-most-likely-to-cheat-at-work-2017-11-17-12881138.

Janofsky, Adam. "You Can Track Employees Working from Home. But Should You?" Protocol. April 29, 2020. https://www.protocol.com/remote-work-boss-tracking-tools.

Komando, Kim. "How to Delete Yourself From the Internet." USA Today. June 23, 2017. https://www.usatoday.com/story/tech/columnist/komando/2017/06/23/how-to-delete-yourself-from-the-internet/102890400/.

Loesche, Dyfed. "Infographic: More Countries Adopt Freedom of Information Laws." Statista Infographics, November 9, 2017. https://www.statista.com/chart/11757/more-countries-adopt-freedom-of-information-laws/.

Manthei, Lisa. "5 Ways Artificial Intelligence Can Be Used in Marketing." Emarsys. April 26, 2017. https://www.emarsys.com/resources/blog/5-ways-artificial-intelligence-can-used-marketing/.

Marvin, Rob. "The Best Employee Monitoring Software for 2020." PCMAG. September 27, 2019. https://www.pcmag.com/picks/the-best-employee-monitoring-software.

Mearian, Lucas. "Bank Offers Virtual Safe-Deposit Boxes for Storing Data." Computerworld. Computerworld, February 19, 2001. https://www.computerworld.com/article/2590794/bank-offers-virtual-safe-deposit-boxes-for-storing-data.html.

Moisejevs, Ilja. "Poisoning Attacks on Machine Learning." Medium. Towards Data Science, July 14, 2019. https://towardsdatascience. com/poisoning-attacks-on-machine-learning-1ff247c254db.

Moisejevs, Ilja. "Poisoning Attacks on Machine Learning." Medium. Towards Data Science. July 15, 2019. https://towardsdatascience. com/poisoning-attacks-on-machine-learning-1ff247c254db.

Myerson, Mark. "Biometric Chips—Are We Ready to Be Microchipped?" Gadget Flow. August 5, 2018. https://thegadget-flow.com/blog/biometric-chips-are-we-ready/.

O'Neil, Cathy. *Weapons of Math Destruction: How Big Data Increases Inequality and Threatens Democracy*. New York, NY: Penguin Books, 2016.

Occupational Health and Safety. "One New Device Tracks Warehouse Worker Movement to Improve Safety." Occupational Health & Safety. November 12, 2019. https://ohsonline.com/arti-cles/2019/11/12/one-new-device-tracks-warehouse-worker-move-ment-to-improve-safety.aspx.

Pearl, Judea, and Dana Mackenzie. 2018. *The Book of Why: The New Science of Cause and Effect*. New York: Basic Books.

Philipps, Dave. "The Military Wants Better Tests for PTSD. Speech Analysis Could Be the Answer." The New York Times Magazine. April 19, 2019. https://www.nytimes.com/2019/04/22/magazine/veterans-ptsd-speech-analysis.html.

Piper, Kelsey. "Exclusive: Google Cancels AI Ethics Board in Response to Outcry." Vox. April 4, 2019. http://www.vox.com/ future-perfect/2019/4/4/18295933/google-cancels-ai-ethics-board.

Premo, L. S., and Jean-Jacques Hublin. "Culture, Population Structure, and Low Genetic Diversity in Pleistocene Hominins." *Proceedings of the National Academy of Sciences* 106, no. 1 (January 6, 2009): 33–37. https://doi.org/10.1073/pnas.0809194105.

Quora. "Is Data More Important Than Algorithms," Forbes. January 26, 2017. https://www.forbes.com/sites/quora/2017/01/26/ is-data-more-important-than-algorithms-in-ai/#2d6d3d1542c1.

Receptiviti. "Understand the People Who Matter to Your Business." Receptiviti, 2020. https://www.receptiviti.com.

Richards, Gregory. "Data Poisoning of AI Initiatives: What is it and what to do about it." Government Analytics Research Institute (GARI) / Institut de Recherche En Analytique Gouvernementale (IRAG). 2019. http://gov-ernmentanalytics.institute/magazine/february-2020/ data-poisoning-of-ai-initiatives-what-is-it-and-what-to-do-about-it/.

Rieger, Sarah. "At Least Two Malls Are Using Facial Recognition Technology to Track Shoppers' Ages and Genders without Telling." CBC News. July 27, 2018. https://www.cbc.ca/news/ canada/calgary/calgary-malls-1.4760964.

Safronova, Valeriya. "An Inside Look at Your Favorite Dating Sites." The New York Times. April 11, 2018. https://www.nytimes. com/2018/04/11/style/match-shaadi-league-farmersonly-dating-apps.html.

Saner, Emine. "Employers Are Monitoring Computers, Toilet Breaks—Even Emotions. Is Your Boss Watching You?" The Guardian. Guardian News and Media, May 14, 2018. https://www.theguardian.com/world/2018/may/14/ is-your-boss-secretly-or-not-so-secretly-watching-you.

Steinhardt, Jacob, Pang Wei Koh, and Percy Liang. "Certified Defenses for Data Poisoning Attacks." Advances in Neural Information Processing Systems. November 24, 2017. https://arxiv.org/ abs/1706.03691.

Stowers, Joshua. "7 Ways Your Work Computer Is Betraying You." Business News Daily. May 1, 2020. https://www.businessnewsdaily. com/7928-work-computer-employee-monitoring.html.

Thompson, Stuart A., and Charlie Warzel. "Twelve Million Phones, One Dataset, Zero Privacy." The New York Times. December 19, 2019. https://www.nytimes.com/interactive/2019/12/19/opinion/ location-tracking-cell-phone.html.

Turing, Alan. "Computing Machinery and Intelligence." Mind 59, 236 (1950): 433–460. http://www.jstor.org/stable/2251299.

United Nations. "Right to Privacy in the Digital Age." OHCHR. United Nations General Assembly, December 18, 2013. https://www. ohchr.org/en/issues/digitalage/pages/digitalageindex.aspx.

University of Vermont. "AI can detect depression in a child's speech." Science Daily. May 6, 2019. https://www.sciencedaily.com/releas- es/2019/05/190506150126.html.

Vanian, Jonathan. "Retail Has Big Hopes for A.I. But Shoppers May Have Other Ideas." Fortune. May 2, 2019. https://fortune.com/2019/04/30/artificial-intelligence-walmart-stores/.

Will.I.Am. "We Need to Own Our Data as a Human Right-and Be Compensated for It." The Economist. The Economist Newspaper, January 21, 2019. https://www.economist.com/open-future/2019/01/21/we-need-to-own-our-data-as-a-human-right-and-be-compensated-for-it.

Wolpe, Toby. "Data Privacy: You May Can It Personal Data But Who Actually Owns It?" ZDNet. June 11, 2015. https://www.zdnet.com/article/data-privacy-you-may-call-it-personal-data-but-who-actually-owns-it/.

WorkScape. "Track Worker Productivity in Real Time with WorkScape." WorkScape. 2020. https://www.panogard.com/employee-computer-monitoring-software.html?ga=en17

www.ingramcontent.com/pod-product-compliance
Lightning Source LLC
Chambersburg PA
CBHW070535220526
45467CB00003B/960